American Invitational Math (AIME) Prepa

MW01292516

Volume 1

http://www.mymathcounts.com/index.php

ACKNOWLEDGEMENTS

We wish to thank the following reviewers for their invaluable solutions, insightful comments, and suggestions for improvements to this book:

Maximus Lu (NY), Anthony Cheng (UT), William Sun (VA), Kevin Wang (CO), Stephan Xie (TX), Cindy Ye (AR); Christopher Chang (WA), Jessica Chen (NC), Jin Cheng (CA), Felix Cui (NE), Dr. Maria Du (OH), Dr. Changyong Feng (NY), Linda Gong (CA), Deepak Haldiya (FL), Dr. Ziying Han (NY), Yanli Huang (NJ), Tommy Hu (MA), Dr. Li Yong (IL), Dr. Li Yin Lin (WA), Latha Philip (Ontario, Canada), Aditya Sharma (IL), Huili Shao (MA), Yiqing Shen (TN), Dr. Yang Wei (TX), Yihan Zhong (CT), and Guihua Zhou (CT).

Yongcheng Chen, Ph.D., Author.

Guiling Chen, Owner, mymathcounts.com, Typesetter, Editor.

Copyright © 2014 by mymathcounts.com. All rights reserved. Printed in the United States of America. Reproduction of any portion of this book without the written permission of the authors is strictly prohibited, except as may be expressly permitted by the U.S. Copyright Act.

ISBN-13: 978-1534980969
ISBN-10: 1534980962

Please contact mymathcounts@gmail.com for suggestions, corrections, or clarifications.

Table of Contents

This page is intentionally left blank.

BASIC KNOWLEDGE

<u>**A prism**</u> is a polyhedron bounded by lateral faces and two parallel planes.

Bases, Lateral Surface, Edges.

The two parallel cross-sections which bound a prism are its bases and the other faces form its lateral surface. The edges are the lines in which its lateral faces meet.

The two parallel faces are congruent polygons.
$ABCD = A'B'C'D'$. $ABCD \parallel A'B'C'D'$.

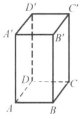

The lateral edges of a prism are equal and parallel.
$AA' = BB'$. $AA' \parallel BB'$.

The lateral faces of a prism are parallelograms.
$ABCD$ is a parallelogram.

<u>**An oblique prism**</u> is a prism whose lateral edges are oblique to the bases.

<u>**A right prism**</u> is a prism whose lateral edges are perpendicular to the bases.

<u>**A regular prism**</u> is a prism whose bases are regular polygons.

The lateral faces are rectangles in a right prism.

A parallelepiped is a prism whose bases, as well as lateral faces, are parallelograms.

A rectangular prism has its bases and all its faces rectangles.
A cube is a parallelepiped whose bases and faces are all squares.

A cross section of a geometric solid is the intersection of a plane and the solid. The cross-sections of a prism made by parallel planes are equal polygons.

Given a prism cut by two parallel planes forming the polygons $ABCDE$ and $A'B'C'D'E'$. $ABCDE = A'B'C'D'E'$.

 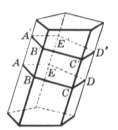

Altitude: The altitude of a prism is the perpendicular distance between the planes of its bases. The altitude of a right prism is equal to its edge.

Area: The lateral area of a prism is the sum of the areas of its lateral faces. The total area is the sum of its lateral area and the areas of its bases.

Volume, V The volume of any prism is equal to the product of its base and altitude.

$V = Bh$
$B =$ base area, $h =$ altitude.

Volume of a rectangular Prism:
$V = abc$

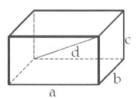

a: length of the base of the solid

b: width of the base of the solid

c: height of the solid

d: space diagonal of the solid, $d^2 = a^2 + b^2 + c^2$.

Surface area of a rectangular Prism, *S*

$S = 2(ab + bc + ca)$

Note: For a cube, $a = b = c$.

Example 1. The side, front, and bottom faces of a rectangular solid have areas of 32, 24, and 48 square units respectively. What is the number of cubic units in the volume of the solid?

Solution: 192 (units^2).

Let the dimensions of the solid be *a*, *b*, and *c*.

$a \times b = 32$ (1)

$b \times c = 24$ (2)

$c \times a = 48$ (3)

$(1) \times (2) \times (3)$:

$(a \times b \times c)^2 = 32 \times 24 \times 48 \quad \Rightarrow \quad a \times b \times c = \sqrt{32 \times 24 \times 48} = 192$.

Example 2. A unit cube has the vertices $ABCD - A'B'C'D'$. Points *L, M, N,* are on the same plane and are the midpoints of *BC, CC',* and *CD,* respectively. The ratio of the surface area of cube to the surface area of the tetrahedron $C-LMN$ can be expressed in simplest radical form as $m(s - \sqrt{n})$, where *m, s,* and *n* are positive integers. Find the sum of *m, s,* and *n*.

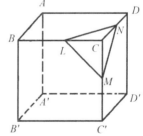

Solution: 014.

The surface area of the cube is $6 \times 1^2 = 6$.

The base of the tetrahedron $C-LMN$ is an equilateral triangle with the side length

of $\sqrt{(\frac{BC}{2})^2 + (\frac{CD}{2})^2} = \frac{\sqrt{2}}{2}$. Its area is $\frac{\sqrt{3}}{4}a^2 = \frac{\sqrt{3}}{4} \times (\frac{\sqrt{2}}{2})^2 = \frac{\sqrt{3}}{8}$.

The surface area of the tetrahedron $C-LMN$ is $\frac{\sqrt{3}}{8} + \frac{1}{8} \times 3 = \frac{\sqrt{3}+3}{8}$.

The ratio is $6 \div \frac{\sqrt{3}+3}{8} = \frac{48}{3+\sqrt{3}} = \frac{48(3-\sqrt{3})}{6} = 8(3-\sqrt{3})$. The answer is $8 + 3 +$

$3 = 14$.

Example 3. The sum of all edges of a rectangular prism is 60. Find the maximum value of the volume.

Solution: 125.

Let x, y, and z be the side lengths of the rectangular prism.

$4(x + y + z) = 60 \qquad \Rightarrow \qquad x + y + z = 15$.

The volume is $V = xyz$.

By $AM-GM$, $V = xyz \le (\frac{x+y+z}{3})^3 = 5^3 = 125$.

The equality holds when $x = y = z = 5$. The answer is 125.

Example 4. A unit cube has the vertices $ABCD - A'B'C'D'$. Points L, M, N, L', M', N' are the midpoints of BC, CD, DD', $D'A'$, $A'B'$, $B'B$, respectively. The areas

of hexagon $LMNL'M'N'$ can be expressed as $\frac{a\sqrt{b}}{c}$, where a, b, c are positive

integers. Find the sum of a, b, and c. a and c are relatively prime.

Solution: 010.

Since $M'L' \,/\!/\, B'D'$, and $NN' \,/\!/\, B'D'$, M', L', N, N'
are on the same plane.

Since $M'M \,/\!/\, A'D$, and $L'N \,/\!/A'D$, M', L', N, M

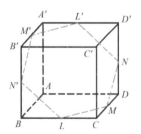

4

are on the same plane.

Since $NM // D'C$, and $L'L // D'C$, N, M, L, L'
are on the same plane.

We see that these three planes share the same three points, so they are the same plane.

Therefore, points L, M, N, L', M', N' are on the same plane.

Let the diagonal of each face of the cube be d.
$M'N' = NL = LM = MN = NL' = L'M' = M'N' = N'L$

$= \frac{1}{2}A'B = \frac{1}{2}d = \frac{\sqrt{2}}{2}.$

So hexagon $LMNL'M'N'$ is a regular hexagon.

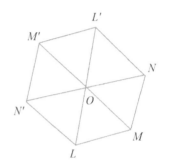

The area is $6 \times \frac{\sqrt{3}}{4}a^2 = 6 \times \frac{\sqrt{3}}{4} \times (\frac{\sqrt{2}}{2})^2 = \frac{3\sqrt{3}}{4}$. the sum is $3 + 3 + 4 = 010$.

Example 5. Given a unit cube $ABCD - EFGH$. From one of the vertices, as A, draw the three surface diagonals meeting at that point. Join the other extremities of these diagonals. These lines are the edges of a new solid $ACFH$, called a regular tetrahedron, or 4−faced solid. The area of the base CFH of the tetrahedron is $\frac{\sqrt{a}}{b}$ and the height is $\frac{c\sqrt{d}}{e}$ in simplest radical form. Find the product of a, b, c, d, and e.

Solution: 108.
The side length of tetrahedron $A-CFH$

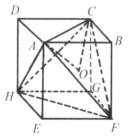

is $\sqrt{2}$. The base CFH is an equilateral triangle with the area $\dfrac{\sqrt{3}}{4} \times (\sqrt{2})^2 = \dfrac{\sqrt{3}}{2}$.

Let the centroid of equilateral triangle CFH be O.

$$CO = \frac{\sqrt{3}}{4}(\sqrt{2}) \times \frac{2}{3} = \sqrt{\frac{2}{3}}.$$

The height $AO = \sqrt{AC^2 - OC^2} = \sqrt{2 - \dfrac{2}{3}} = \dfrac{2\sqrt{3}}{3}$.

The answer is $3 \times 2 \times 2 \times 3 \times 3 = 108$.

Example 6. As shown in the figure, the cube has the side length of $100\sqrt{3}$. Find the distance from the plane DEG to the plane ACF.

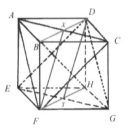

Solution: 100.
We know that BF is $\perp$ to the plane ABC. So $BF \perp AC$.

We know that $BD \perp AC$. Thus AC is $\perp$ to the plane $BDHF$. Line BH is in the plane $BDHF$. So $AC \perp BH$.

Similarly, $CF \perp BH$. Then we know that BH is $\perp$ to the plane ACF.

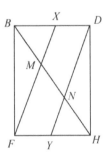

Similarly, $BH \perp DE$, $BH \perp DG$. Then we know that BH is $\perp$ to the plane DEG.

Connect BD. BD meets AC at X.
Connect FH. FH meets EG at Y.

X and Y are midpoints of sides BD and FH of the rectangle $BFHD$, respectively.

Connect FX. FX meets BH at M.

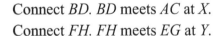

Connect *DY*. *DY* meets *BH* at *N*.
M and *N* trisect *BH*.

Since *M* and *N* are the interesting points of *BH* with the planes *ACF* and *DEG*,
MN is the distance from the plane *DEG* to the plane *ACF*.

So $MN = \frac{1}{3}BH = \frac{\sqrt{3}}{3}a = \frac{\sqrt{3}}{3} \times 100\sqrt{3} = 100$.

Example 7. An octahedron is formed by joining the centers of adjoining faces of
a 10 cm × 15 cm × 20 cm rectangular prism. Find the volume of the octahedron.

Solution: 500.
P, Q, R, S, V, V' are the center of faces *ABCD, ABB'A',*
A'B' C'D', CC'D'D, ADD'A', BCC'B', respectively.
Let *AB = a, BC = b,* and *BB' = c*.

Since the plane *PQRS* ⊥ *VV'*, its area is $\frac{1}{2}bc$.

We know that *VV' = a*, The volume of the octahedron is

$\frac{1}{3} \times (\frac{1}{2}bc) \times a = \frac{1}{6}abc = \frac{1}{6} \times 10 \times 15 \times 20 = 500$.

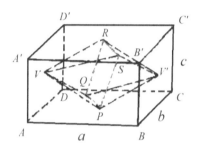

☆**Example 8.** Three of the vertices of a cube are *P* = (6, 11, 10), *Q* = (7, 7, 1)
and *R* = (10, 2 , 9) are three vertices of a cube. Find the volume of the cube.

Solution: 343.
Δ*PQR* is an equilateral triangle.
$PQ = \sqrt{(7-6)^2 + (7-11)^2 + (1-10)^2}$
$= \sqrt{1+16+81} = 7\sqrt{2}$.
The side length of the cube is then *x* = 7.
The volume of the cube is $7^3 = 343$.

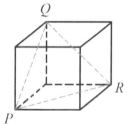

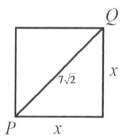

Example 9. (1988 IMO Longlist Modified) Suppose that $ABCD$ and $EFGH$ are opposite faces of a rectangular solid, with $\angle DHC = 45°$ and $\angle FHB = 60°$. Find the cosine of $\angle BHD$.

Solution: $\dfrac{\sqrt{6}}{4}$.

Let $AB = 1$.

We know that $\angle DHC$ is 45°. So $CDGH$ is also a square with $DH = \sqrt{2}$.

We are given that $\angle FHB = 60°$. We see that $FB = HC = CD = AB = 1$. So $HB = \dfrac{2}{\sqrt{3}}$.

Since $HC = CD$, $DB = HB = \dfrac{2}{\sqrt{3}}$.

Applying the law of cosine to triangle HBD,

$$\cos \angle BHD = \frac{(\sqrt{2})^2 + (\frac{2}{\sqrt{3}})^2 - (\frac{2}{\sqrt{3}})^2}{2 \times \sqrt{2} \times \frac{2}{\sqrt{3}}} = \frac{\sqrt{6}}{4}.$$

☆**Example 10**. A 12 cm × 12 cm square is divided into two pieces by joining to adjacent side midpoints, as shown in the first figure. Copies of the triangular piece are placed on alternate edges of a regular hexagon with the side length of $6\sqrt{2}$ and copies of the other piece are placed on the other edges, as shown in the first figure. The resulting figure is then folded to give a polyhedron with 7 faces. What is the volume of the polyhedron?

(1)

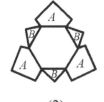
(2)

Solution: 864.

Method 1:

The original solid is a cube with the side length 10 cm. The volume of the 7-faces polyhedron is half of the volume of the cube.

The answer is $12^3 / 2 = 864$ cm^3.

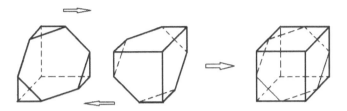

Method 2:

The original solid is a tetrahedron with the side length 18 cm. The volume of the

7-faces polyhedron is $V = \dfrac{1}{3} \times \dfrac{1}{2} \times 18^3 - 3 \times \dfrac{1}{3} \times \dfrac{1}{2} \times 6^3 = 864$.

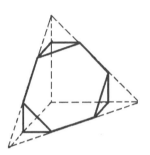

PROBLEMS

Problem 1. The side, front, and bottom faces of a rectangular solid have areas of $\sqrt{3}$, $\sqrt{5}$, and $\sqrt{15}$ square units, respectively. What is the number of units in the length of the space diagonal of the solid?

Problem 2. For one vertex of a solid cube with the side length of 2, consider the tetrahedron formed by the vertex and the midpoints of three edges that meet at that vertex. The surface area of the portion of the cube that remains when the tetrahedron is cut away can be expressed as $\dfrac{a+\sqrt{b}}{c}$ in simplest radical form. Find the value of $a + b + c$.

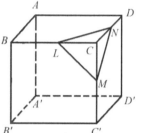

Problem 3. The sum of all edges of a rectangular prism is 60. Find the maximum value of the surface area of the rectangular prism.

Problem 4. The ratio of the length to width to height of a rectangular prism is 4:3:2. The space diagonal of the rectangular prism is the same as the space diagonal of a cube. The ratio of the surface areas of the rectangular prism to the surface area of the cube is $a:b$, where a and b are positive integers relatively prime. Find the sum of a and b.

Problem 5. A rectangular box is 5 inches long, 4 inches wide, and 2 inches high. The vertices are $ABCD - A'B'C'D'$. Points L, M, N, L', M', N' are on the same plane and are the midpoints of $BC, CD, DD', D'A', A'B', B'B$, respectively. The ratio of the area of the hexagon $LMNL'M'N'$ to the area of the triangle $A'BD$ can be expressed as $\dfrac{a}{b}$, where a and b are positive integers relatively prime. Find the

sum of a and b.

Problem 6. A rectangular prism with volume 32 cm^3 and height 2 cm has the
vertices $ABCD$-$EFGH$. Connect the vertices of BEG to form
a tetrahedron $FBEG$ with the base BEG. The maximum

distance from F to the base BEG can be expressed as $\dfrac{a\sqrt{b}}{c}$

in simplest radical form. Find the product of a, b, and c.

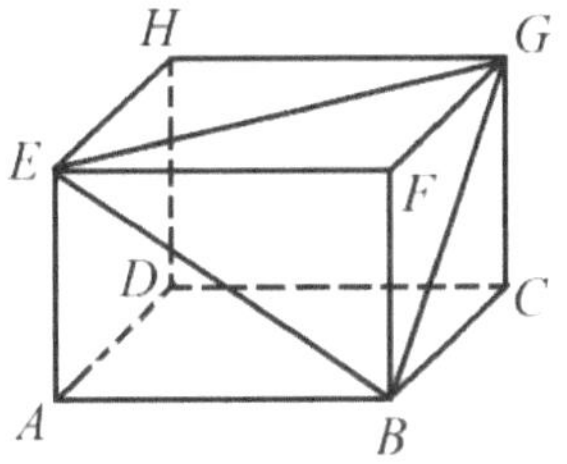

Problem 7. A rectangular prism has the side lengths a, b, and c. A tetrahedron
$P-A'B'C'$ is formed as shown in the figure with the base
$A'B'C'$. Find PH, the distance from P to the base $A'B'C'$.

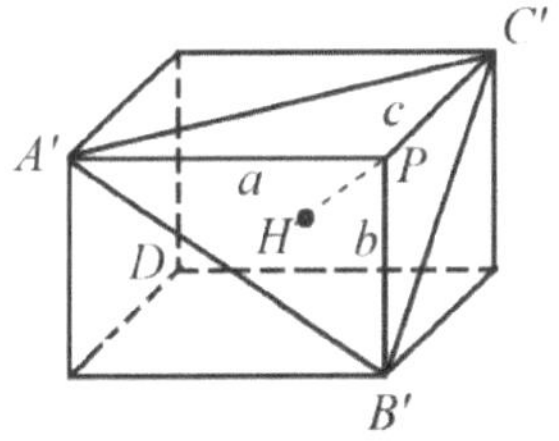

Problem 8. As shown in the figure, the rectangular prism has the dimensions AA'
= 4, $A'B'$ = 8, and $A'D'$ = 16. Points M, N, P, Q are the midpoints of $A'B'$, $D'A'$,
BC, CD, respectively. Find the distance between the
centroids of $\triangle AMN$ and $\triangle C'PQ$.

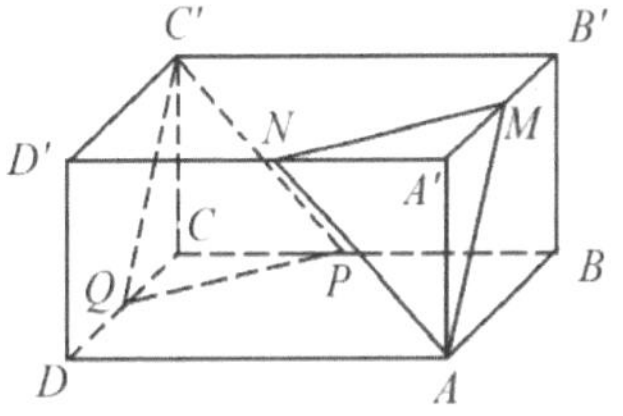

11

Problem 9. A tetrahedron $D-ACH$ is formed by joining the vertices of ACH of a rectangular prism with the square base. The surface area of the tetrahedron $DACH$ is $\sqrt{3}+3$. $\angle AHC = 60°$. Find the surface area of the rectangular prism.

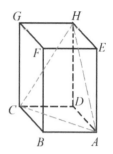

Problem 10. Given a cube $ABCD - A'B'C'D'$. E is the midpoint of the edge BB'. F is a point on BC. Find $\angle D'EF$ if $C'E \perp EF$.

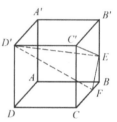

Problem 11. Given a rectangular prism $ABCD - A'B'C'D'$. $AB = AD$. $AA' = 2AB$. The cosine of the angle formed by $A'B$ and AD' can be expressed as $\dfrac{a}{b}$. Find the sum of a and b if a and b are relatively prime.

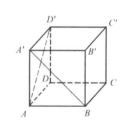

✰**Problem 12 (1986 AIME)** The shortest distances between an interior diagonal of a rectangular parallelepiped (box), P, and the edges it does not meet are $2\sqrt{5}$, $\dfrac{30}{\sqrt{13}}$, and $\dfrac{15}{\sqrt{10}}$. Determine the volume of P.

Problem 13. The space diagonal of a rectangular box is $8\sqrt{2}$. The angle formed by the space diagonal and the base of the rectangular box is 30°. The angle formed by the two diagonal of the base is 45. Find the volume of the rectangular box.

Problem 14. The space diagonal of a rectangular box is l. The angle formed by the space diagonal and the base of the rectangular box is α. The angle formed by the two diagonal of the base is β. Find the volume of the rectangular box.

SOLUTIONS

Problem 1. Solution: 003.
Let the dimensions of the solid be a, b, and c, and the length of the space diagonal is l.

$$a \times b = \sqrt{3} \qquad\qquad\qquad\qquad\qquad (1)$$
$$b \times c = \sqrt{5} \qquad\qquad\qquad\qquad\qquad (2)$$
$$c \times a = \sqrt{15} \qquad\qquad\qquad\qquad\qquad (3)$$

Method 1:
(1) × (2) × (3):
$$(a \times b \times c)^2 = \sqrt{3} \times \sqrt{5} \times \sqrt{15} \qquad \Rightarrow \qquad a \times b \times c = \sqrt{15} \qquad (4)$$
(4) ÷ (1): $c = \sqrt{5}$.
(4) ÷ (2): $a = \sqrt{3}$.
(4) ÷ (3): $b = 1$.
$$l = \sqrt{a^2 + b^2 + c^2} = \sqrt{3+1+5} = \sqrt{9} = 3.$$

Method 2 (by Cindy Ye):
(1) × (2): $a \times b^2 \times c = \sqrt{3} \times \sqrt{5} = \sqrt{15} \qquad\qquad\qquad (4)$
Substituting (3) into (4): $a \times b^2 \times c = a \times c \quad \Rightarrow \quad b^2 = 1$.
So $b = 1$. We then get $a = \sqrt{3}$ and $c = \sqrt{5}$.
$$l = \sqrt{a^2 + b^2 + c^2} = \sqrt{3+1+5} = \sqrt{9} = 3.$$

Problem 2. Solution: 050.
As shown in the figure, the cube is $ABCD - A'B'C'D'$. Points L, M, N are the midpoints of BC, CC', and CD, respectively.

The tetrahedron $C-LMN'$ base is an equilateral triangle with

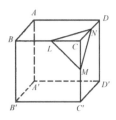

14

the side length of $\sqrt{(\frac{BC}{2})^2 + (\frac{CD}{2})^2} = \sqrt{2}$.

Its area is $\dfrac{\sqrt{3}}{4}a^2 = \dfrac{\sqrt{3}}{4} \times (\sqrt{2})^2 = \dfrac{\sqrt{3}}{2}$.

The lateral surface area of the tetrahedron $C–LMN$ is $\dfrac{1}{2} \times 3 = \dfrac{3}{2}$.

The surface area of the portion of the cube that remains is

$6 \times 4 - \dfrac{3}{2} + \dfrac{\sqrt{3}}{2} = \dfrac{45 + \sqrt{3}}{2}$.

The answer is $45 + 3 + 2 = 50$.

Problem 3. Solution: 150.

Let x, y, and z be the side lengths of the rectangular prism.

$4(x + y + z) = 60 \qquad \Rightarrow \qquad x + y + z = 15$.

The surface area is $S = 2(xy + yz + zx)$

We know that $(x + y + z)^2 = x^2 + y^2 + z^2 + 2(xy + yz + zx)$.

$2(xy + yz + zx) = (x + y + z)^2 - (x^2 + y^2 + z^2)$.

By Cauchy, $x^2 + y^2 + z^2 \geq \dfrac{(x + y + z)^2}{3} = 75$.

The smallest value of is 75 when $x = y = z = 5$.

When $x^2 + y^2 + z^2$ has the smallest value, $2(xy + yz + zx)$ has the maximum value, which is $15^2 - 75 = 150$.

Problem 4. Solution: 055.

Let the length, width, and height of the rectangular prism be $4x$, $3x$, and $2x$, respectively.

The space diagonal is $d_1 = \sqrt{(4x)^2 + (3x)^2 + (2x)^2} = \sqrt{29}x$.

The space diagonal of the cube is $d_2 = \sqrt{3}y = \sqrt{29}x$. y is the side of the cube.

$y = \dfrac{\sqrt{29}}{\sqrt{3}}x$.

The surface area of the rectangular prism is $2(4x \times 3x + 3x \times 2x + 2x \times 4x) = 52x^2$.

The surface area of the cube is $6y^2 = 6 \times (\frac{\sqrt{29}}{\sqrt{3}})^2 = 58x^2$.

The ratio is $52:58 = 26:29$. The answer is $26 + 29 = 55$.

Problem 5. Solution: 005.

$M'N' = NM = \frac{1}{2}A'B$, $N'L = L'N = \frac{1}{2}A'D$,

$LM = L'M = \frac{1}{2}BD$.

$S_{M'N'OL'} = S_{N'LMO} = S_{MNL'O} = \frac{1}{2}S_{\triangle A'BD}$.

The ratio of the areas of hexagon $LMNL'M'N'$ and triangle $A'BD$ is:

$\frac{3S_{MNL'O}}{S_{\triangle A'BD}} = \frac{3}{2}$.

The sum is $2 + 3 = 005$.

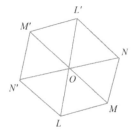
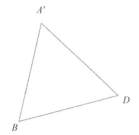

Problem 6. Solution: 036.

Draw $FM \perp EG$ at M in the plane $EFGH$. Connect BM. Let d be the distance from F to the base BEG.

Let $AB = x$ and $BC = y$.

We know that the edge BF is $\perp$ to the plane $EFGH$. We also know that $FM \perp EG$. Thus $BM \perp EG$.

The volume of the tetrahedron $FBEG$ can be expressed in the following two ways:

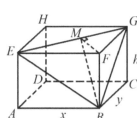

$$\frac{1}{3}S_{\triangle BEG} \cdot d = \frac{1}{3}S_{\triangle EFG} \cdot BF \quad \Rightarrow \quad d = \frac{\frac{1}{3}S_{\triangle EFG} \cdot BF}{\frac{1}{3}S_{\triangle BEG}} = \frac{S_{\triangle EFG} \cdot h}{S_{\triangle BEG}} \text{ or}$$

16

$$d = \frac{\frac{1}{2}EG \cdot MF}{\frac{1}{2}EG \cdot BM} \cdot h = \frac{MF}{BM} \cdot h = \frac{MF}{\sqrt{BF^2 + MF^2}} \cdot h = \frac{MF \cdot h}{\sqrt{h^2 + MF^2}}.$$

Squaring both sides: $d^2 = \frac{MF^2 \cdot h^2}{h^2 + MF^2}$ $\Rightarrow$ $\frac{1}{d^2} = \frac{h^2 + MF^2}{h^2 \cdot MF^2} = \frac{1}{MF^2} + \frac{1}{h^2}$ (1)

The area of the right triangle EFG can be expressed in the following two ways:

$$\frac{1}{2}EG \cdot MF = \frac{1}{2}EF \cdot FG \qquad \Rightarrow \qquad MF = \frac{EF \cdot FG}{EG} \text{ or}$$

$$MF = \frac{xy}{\sqrt{x^2 + y^2}} = \frac{xyh}{h\sqrt{x^2 + y^2}} = \frac{V}{h\sqrt{x^2 + y^2}}. \text{ Thus } \frac{1}{MF^2} = \frac{h^2(x^2 + y^2)}{V^2}.$$

We know that $x^2 + y^2 \geq 2xy$. The equality holds when $x = y$.

Thus $\frac{1}{MF^2} \geq \frac{h^2 2xy}{V^2} = \frac{2h}{V}$ (2)

The equality holds when $x = y$.

From (1) and (2), we get: $\frac{1}{d^2} \geq \frac{2h}{V} + \frac{1}{h^2} = \frac{2h^3 + V}{Vh^2}$ $\Rightarrow$ $d \leq h\sqrt{\frac{V}{2h^3 + V}}.$

When $ABCD$ is a square, the maximum distance from F to the base BEG can be

expressed $d = h\sqrt{\frac{V}{2h^3 + V}}$, or $d = 2 \times \sqrt{\frac{32}{2 \times 2^3 + 32}} = \frac{2\sqrt{6}}{3}$. The answer is $2 \times 6 \times$

$3 = 36$.

Problem 7. Solution:

Applying the law of cosine to triangle $A'B'C'$:

$$\cos \angle A'C'B' = \frac{C'A'^2 + C'B'^2 - A'B'^2}{2C'A' \cdot C'B'} =$$

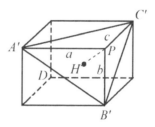

$$\frac{(c^2 + a^2) + (c^2 + b^2) - (a^2 + b^2)}{2\sqrt{(c^2 + a^2)(c^2 + b^2)}} = \frac{c^2}{\sqrt{(c^2 + a^2)(c^2 + b^2)}}.$$

So $\sin \angle A'C'B' = \dfrac{\sqrt{a^2b^2 + b^2c^2 + c^2a^2}}{\sqrt{(c^2 + a^2)(c^2 + b^2)}}$.

So $S_{\triangle A'B'C'} = \dfrac{1}{2}C'A' \times C'B' \sin \angle A'C'B' = \dfrac{1}{2}\sqrt{a^2b^2 + b^2c^2 + c^2a^2}$.

We know that $V_{P-A'B'C'} = \dfrac{1}{6}abc$.

Therefore $\dfrac{1}{3}S_{\triangle A'B'C'} \times PH = \dfrac{1}{6}abc \Rightarrow PH = \dfrac{\dfrac{1}{6}abc}{\dfrac{1}{3}S_{\triangle A'B'C'}} = \dfrac{abc}{2S_{\triangle A'B'C'}} = $

$\dfrac{abc}{\sqrt{a^2b^2 + b^2c^2 + c^2a^2}}$.

Problem 8. Solution: 012.

Let rectangle $A'C'CA$ meet the plane AMN at AX and the plane $C'PQ$ at $C'Y$. Then AX is the median of $\triangle AMN$ and $C'Y$ is the median of $\triangle C'PQ$.

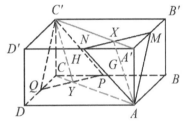

Let the centroids of $\triangle AMN$ and $\triangle C'PQ$ be G and H. The projections of them are G_x, H_x, and G_y, H_y on AC, CC', respectively.

So $G_y H_y = \dfrac{4}{3}$.

Then $G_y H_y = \dfrac{4}{3}$. $G_x H_x = (1 - 2\dfrac{2}{3} \times \dfrac{1}{4})\sqrt{8^2 + 16^2} = \dfrac{2}{3}\sqrt{320}$.

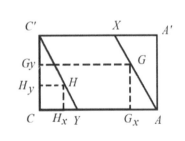

$GH = \sqrt{(\dfrac{4}{3})^2 + (\dfrac{2}{3}\sqrt{320})^2} = \sqrt{\dfrac{16}{9} + \dfrac{4 \times 320}{9}}$

$= \sqrt{\dfrac{1296}{9}} = \sqrt{144} = 12.$

Problem 9. Solution: 012.

Let a be the side length of the rectangle $ABCD$. $AC = \sqrt{2}a$.

We see that $AH = HC$, $\angle AHC = 60°$. Thus $\triangle AHC$ is an equilateral triangle. So

$AH = HC\ AC = \sqrt{2}a$. $DH = a$. So this rectangular prism is a cube. The surface area is $6a^2$.

Let the surface area of the tetrahedron $D-ACH$ be S.

$$S = S_{\triangle AHC} + 3 \times \frac{a^2}{2} = \frac{\sqrt{3}}{4} \times (\sqrt{2}a)^2 + 3 \times \frac{a^2}{2} = \frac{1}{2}a^2(3 + \sqrt{3}).$$

Therefore $\dfrac{1}{2}a^2(3 + \sqrt{3}) = \sqrt{3} + 3 \quad \Rightarrow \quad a^2 = 2$.

The surface area of the rectangular prism is $6a^2 = 6 \times 2 = 12$.

Problem 10. Solution: 090.

Since $\angle C'EF = 90°$, $\triangle C'B'E \sim \triangle EBF$. So $\dfrac{C'E}{EF} = \dfrac{B'E}{BF} = \dfrac{C'B'}{EB}$.

Let the side length of the cube be 1. Then $C'B' = 1$. $B'E = \dfrac{1}{2}$.

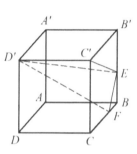

$C'E = \dfrac{\sqrt{5}}{2}$. $EB = \dfrac{1}{2}$.

Thus $BF = \dfrac{1}{4}$. $EF = \dfrac{\sqrt{5}}{4}$. $CF = \dfrac{3}{4}$.

In right triangle $D'C'E$, $D'E = \sqrt{1^2 + (\dfrac{\sqrt{5}}{2})^2} = \dfrac{3}{2}$.

In right triangle $D'C'F$, $D'F = \sqrt{(\sqrt{2})^2 + (\dfrac{3}{4})^2} = \dfrac{\sqrt{41}}{4}$.

$$\cos \angle D'EF = \frac{(\dfrac{3}{2})^2 + (\dfrac{\sqrt{5}}{4})^2 - (\dfrac{\sqrt{41}}{4})^2}{2 \times \dfrac{3}{2} \times \dfrac{\sqrt{5}}{4}} = 0 \quad \Rightarrow \quad \angle D'EF = 90°.$$

Problem 11. Solution: 009.

Connect $D'C$ and AC. We know that $A'B \parallel D'C$.

The solution is to find cos $AD'C$.

Let $AB = 1$. Then $AA' = 2$. $AD' = D'C = \sqrt{5}$. $AC = \sqrt{2}$.

Applying the law of cosine to triangle $AD'C$,

$$\cos \angle AD'C = \frac{(\sqrt{5})^2 + (\sqrt{5})^2 - (\sqrt{2})^2}{2 \times \sqrt{5} \times \sqrt{5}} = \frac{4}{5}.$$

The answer is $4 + 5 = 9$.

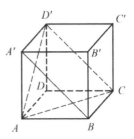

☆Problem 12 (1986 AIME) Solution: 750.

The space diagonal is $D'B$.

Let the three edges of the rectangular box be $A'D' = a$, $A'A = b$, $AB = c$.

We first find the shortest distance from edges $A'A$ that does not meet $D'B$ to $A'B'$.

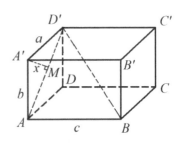

Connect AD'. Draw the height from A' to $A'D$ to meet AD' at M. We see that the height $A'M$ is exactly the distance from $A'B'$ to $D'B$.

We write the area of triangle $A'AD'$ in two ways: $\frac{1}{2} A'A \times A'D' = \frac{1}{2} AD' \times x$ $\Rightarrow$

$$b \times a = (\sqrt{a^2 + b^2}) \times x.$$

Solving for x: $x = \dfrac{ab}{\sqrt{a^2 + b^2}}$. Similarly we get:

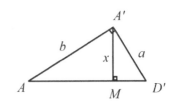

$y = \dfrac{bc}{\sqrt{b^2 + c^2}}$ and $z = \dfrac{ca}{\sqrt{c^2 + a^2}}$.

Solving the system of equations:

$$\frac{ab}{\sqrt{a^2 + b^2}} = 2\sqrt{5} \Rightarrow \frac{a^2 b^2}{a^2 + b^2} = 20 \Rightarrow \frac{a^2 + b^2}{a^2 b^2} = \frac{1}{20} \Rightarrow \frac{1}{a^2} + \frac{1}{b^2} = \frac{1}{20} \quad (1)$$

$$\frac{bc}{\sqrt{b^2 + c^2}} = \frac{30}{\sqrt{13}} \Rightarrow \frac{b^2 c^2}{b^2 + c^2} = \frac{900}{13} \Rightarrow \frac{1}{b^2} + \frac{1}{c^2} = \frac{13}{900} \quad (2)$$

$$\frac{ca}{\sqrt{c^2 + a^2}} = \frac{15}{\sqrt{10}} \Rightarrow \frac{c^2 a^2}{c^2 + a^2} = \frac{45}{2} \Rightarrow \frac{1}{c^2} + \frac{1}{a^2} = \frac{2}{45} \quad (3)$$

Solving we get $a = 5$, $b = 10$, and $c = 15$. The volume is 750.

Problem 13. Solution: 192.
Let O be the intersection of base diagonals AC and BD.
$\angle AOD = 45°$. $\angle D'BD = 30°$.
In right triangle $D'DB$, $D'D = D'B \times \sin 30° =$

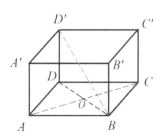

$\dfrac{1}{2} \times 8\sqrt{2} = 4\sqrt{2}$.

$BD = D'B \times \cos 30° = \dfrac{\sqrt{3}}{2} \times 8\sqrt{2} = 4\sqrt{6}$.

So $AO = DO = \dfrac{1}{2} BD = \dfrac{\sqrt{3}}{4} \times 8\sqrt{2} = 2\sqrt{6}$.

$S_{ABCD} = 4S_{\triangle AOD} = 4 \times \dfrac{1}{2} AO \times DO \times \sin 45° = 4 \times \dfrac{1}{2} \times (2\sqrt{6})^2 \times \dfrac{\sqrt{2}}{2} = 24\sqrt{2}$.

the volume of the rectangular box is $V = S_{ABCD} \times D'D = 24\sqrt{2} \times 4\sqrt{2} = 192$.

Problem 14. Solution:
Let O be the intersection of base diagonals AC and BD.
$\angle AOD = \beta$. $\angle ECA = \alpha$.
In right triangle ECA, $EA = l \sin \alpha$. $AC = l \cos \alpha$.

So $AO = BO = CO = DO = \dfrac{1}{2} l \cos \alpha$.

The area of rectangle $ABCD$

$S_{ABCD} = 2S_{\triangle ADC} = 4S_{\triangle AOD} = 4 \times \dfrac{1}{2} AO \times DO \times \sin \beta = 2 \times (\dfrac{1}{2} l \cos \alpha)^2 \times \sin \beta$

$= \dfrac{1}{2} l^2 \times \cos^2 \alpha \times \sin \beta$.

The volume of the rectangular box is $V = S_{ABCD} \times EA = \dfrac{1}{2} l^2 \times \cos^2 \alpha \times \sin \beta$

$\times l \sin \alpha$

$= \dfrac{1}{2} l^3 \times \cos^2 \alpha \times \sin \alpha \times \sin \beta$.

BASIC KNOWLEDGE

Similar triangles are triangles whose corresponding angles are congruent and whose corresponding sides are in proportion to each other. Similar triangles have the same shape but are not necessarily the same size.

The symbol for "similar" is ~. The notation $\Delta ABC \sim \Delta A'B'C'$ is read as "triangle ABC is similar to triangle A-prime B-prime C-prime."

Principles of Similar Triangles

Principle 1. *(AA)* If two angles of one triangle are congruent respectively to two angles of the other triangle, the two triangles are similar by *AA* (angle, angle).

Corollary of Principle 2: Two right triangles are similar if they have one congruent acute angle.

Principle 2. (*SAS*) If two sides of one triangle are proportional to the corresponding parts of another triangle, and the ***included*** angles are congruent, the two triangles are similar by *SAS* (side, angle, side).

If $\dfrac{a}{c} = \dfrac{b}{d}$ and $\alpha = \beta$, then two triangles are similar.

Principle 3. (*SSS*) If three corresponding sides (segments) of two triangles are in proportion , the two triangles are similar by *SSS* (side, side, side).

If $\dfrac{a}{a_1} = \dfrac{b}{b_1} = \dfrac{c}{c_1}$, then $\Delta ABC \sim \Delta A_1 B_1 C_1$.

Principle 4. (HL) If the corresponding hypotenuse and one leg of two right triangles are in proportion , the two triangles are similar by *HL* (hypotenuse, leg).

Theorem 1. Corresponding sides (segments) of similar triangles are in proportion to each other.

If $\triangle ABC \sim \triangle A_1B_1C_1$, then $\dfrac{a}{a_1} = \dfrac{b}{b_1} = \dfrac{c}{c_1}$

and the ratio of the areas is as follows:

$$\frac{S_{\triangle ABC}}{S_{\triangle A_1B_1C_1}} = (\frac{a}{a_1})^2 = (\frac{b}{b_1})^2 = (\frac{c}{c_1})^2$$

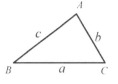 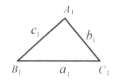

Theorem 2. A line parallel to a side of a triangle cuts off a triangle similar to the given triangle.

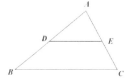

If *DE//BC*, then $\triangle ABC \sim \triangle ADE$

$$\frac{AD}{AB} = \frac{AE}{AC} = \frac{DE}{BC}$$

$$\frac{AD}{DB} = \frac{AE}{EC} \quad \Rightarrow \quad \frac{AD}{AE} = \frac{DB}{EC}$$

Theorem 3. If $\angle ACB = \angle ADC = 90°$, then

$$AC^2 = AB \times AD \qquad (1)$$
$$BC^2 = AB \times BD \qquad (2)$$
$$CD^2 = AD \times BD \qquad (3)$$
$$CD \times AB = AC \times BC \qquad (4)$$

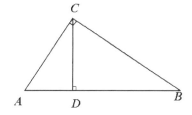

PROBLEMS INVOLVED IN ONE OR TWO PAIRS OF TRIANGLES

☆ **Example 1.** In rectangle $ABCD$, $AB = 50\sqrt{6}$. Let E be the midpoint of AD. What is the largest integer less than AD if lines AC and BE are perpendicular?

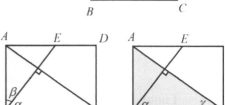

Solution: 173.
As shown in the figures, we see that $\alpha + \beta = 90°$ and
$\alpha + \gamma = 90°$. Thus $\beta = \gamma$.
$\Delta BAE \sim \Delta CBA$.

$$\frac{AB}{BC} = \frac{AE}{AB} \quad \Rightarrow \quad \frac{50\sqrt{6}}{2AE} = \frac{AE}{50\sqrt{6}}$$

$$\Rightarrow \quad \sqrt{2}AE = 50\sqrt{6}$$

$$\Rightarrow \quad \sqrt{2} \times \sqrt{2}AE = 50\sqrt{6} \times \sqrt{2} \quad \Rightarrow$$

$$2AE = AD = 100\sqrt{3}.$$

Since $173 < 100\sqrt{3} < 174$, the answer is 173.

☆**Example 2.** As shown in the figure, $ABCD$ is a square with $AB = 1$. Four points E, F, G, H lie on sides AB, CD, DA, respectively, with $AE = BF = CG = DH$. The area of the shaded small square to the area of $ABCD$ can be

expressed as $\dfrac{1}{2113}$. What is the value of $\dfrac{1}{BE}$?

Solution: 033.
Draw $EK \perp BG$ at K. Let J be the point of intersection of AF and
BG. $x = 1/BE$.
Right triangle $BKE \sim BAF$ ($\angle BEK = \angle BAJ$, $\angle BJA = \angle BKE = 90°$).

$$\frac{AB}{EK} = \frac{BF}{BK} \quad \Rightarrow \quad \frac{1}{\dfrac{1}{\sqrt{2113}}} = \frac{1 - \dfrac{1}{x}}{\sqrt{\dfrac{1}{x^2} - (\dfrac{1}{\sqrt{2113}})^2}}$$

$$\Rightarrow \sqrt{2113} = \frac{\dfrac{x-1}{x}}{\sqrt{\dfrac{1}{x^2}-\dfrac{1}{2113}}} \Rightarrow$$

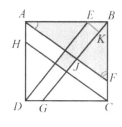

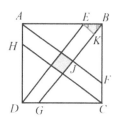

$$\sqrt{2113} = \frac{\dfrac{x-1}{x}}{\dfrac{\sqrt{2113-x^2}}{x\sqrt{2113}}} \Rightarrow$$

$$\sqrt{2113-x^2} = x-1 \Rightarrow 2113-x^2 = (x-1)^2$$

$x = 33$ or $x = -32$ (ignored).

☆**Example 3:** (1984 AIME) A point P is chosen in the interior of $\triangle ABC$ so that when lines are drawn through P parallel to the sides of $\triangle ABC$, the resulting smaller triangles, t_1, t_2 and t_3 in the figure, have areas 4, 9 and 49, respectively. Find the area of $\triangle ABC$.

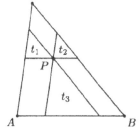

Solution: 144.

Method 1:
Let R and T be the two points that the lines drawn parallel through P intersect with AB, with R being the point closer to A.

The ratio of the corresponding sides of areas t_1, t_2 and t_3 is:
$$PM : PN : RT = \sqrt{4} : \sqrt{9} : \sqrt{49} = 2:3:7.$$

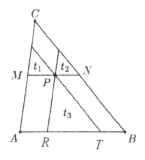

Or $AR : RT : BT = 2:3:7$.
$AB : RT = 12:7$.
$$S_{\triangle ABC} : S_{\triangle PRT} = (AB:RT)^2 = 12^2 : 7^2.$$
Therefore $S_{\triangle ABC} = \dfrac{144}{49} \times 49 = 144$.

Method 2 (our solution):

Let the area of $\triangle ABC$ be S. We know that t_1, t_2, t_3 are all similar to $\triangle ABC$ and we label each side of the triangles as shown in the figure.

We use the triangle t_2 ($\triangle PNQ$) in our calculation (t_1 or t_3 can also be used):

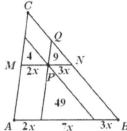

$$\frac{9}{S} = \left(\frac{3x}{12x}\right)^2 \quad \Rightarrow \quad \frac{9}{S} = \left(\frac{1}{4}\right)^2 = \frac{1}{16} \Rightarrow \quad S = 9 \times 16 = 144.$$

☆ **Example 4:** In $\triangle ABC$ shown below, $AB = 34$, $BC = 51$ and $CA = 68$. Moreover, P is an interior point chosen so that the segments DE, FG and HI are each of length d, contain P, and are parallel to the sides AB, BC and CA, respectively. Given that $d = p/q$, where p and q are relatively prime positive integers, find $p + q$.

Solution: 419.

$EH = BC - (BE + HC) = BC - (FP + PG) = 51 - d.$

Similarly $GD = 68 - d$.

We know that $\triangle DPG \sim \triangle ABC$, so $\dfrac{DP}{AB} = \dfrac{GD}{CA}$

$$\Rightarrow DP = \frac{GD}{CA} \cdot AB = \frac{68 - D}{68} \cdot 34 = 34 - \frac{1}{2}d.$$

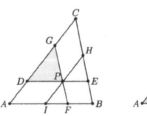 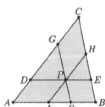

We also know that $\triangle PEH \sim \triangle ABC$.

Therefore $\dfrac{PE}{AB} = \dfrac{EH}{BC}$

$$\Rightarrow PE = \frac{EH}{BC} \cdot AB = \frac{51 - d}{51} \cdot 34 = 34 - \frac{2}{3}d.$$

Hence $d = DP + PE = 68 - \dfrac{5}{6}d \Rightarrow d = 408/11.$

The answer is $408 + 11 = 419.$

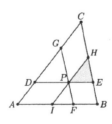 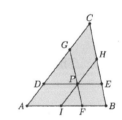

Example 5. As shown in the figure, a point P is chosen in the interior of $\triangle ABC$ and lines are drawn through P parallel to the sides of $\triangle ABC$.

Show that $\dfrac{DE}{BC} + \dfrac{FG}{CA} + \dfrac{LH}{AB} = 2.$

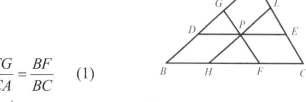

Proof:

We know that $\triangle BFG \sim \triangle BCA$, so $\dfrac{FG}{CA} = \dfrac{BF}{BC}$ (1)

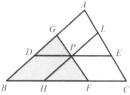 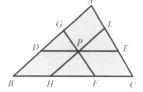

We know that $\triangle CHL \sim \triangle CBA$, so $\dfrac{LH}{AB} = \dfrac{CH}{BC}$ (2)

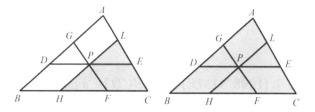

Then we can have: $\dfrac{DE}{BC} + \dfrac{FG}{CA} + \dfrac{LH}{AB} = \dfrac{DE}{BC} + \dfrac{BF}{BC} + \dfrac{CH}{BC} = \dfrac{DE + BF + CH}{BC}$

We see that $DE = DP + PE = BH + FC$. So $\dfrac{DE}{BC} + \dfrac{FG}{CA} + \dfrac{LH}{AB} =$

$\dfrac{BH + FC + BF + CH}{BC} = \dfrac{(BH + CH) + (FC + BF)}{BC} = \dfrac{2BC}{BC} = 2$

Example 6: (1997 China Shandong Province Middle School Math Contest) As shown in the figure below, $ABCD$ is a parallelogram. $A, E, F,$ and G are on the same line. BD is the diagonal. Which one of the following is true?
(A) $AE^2 = EF \times FG$

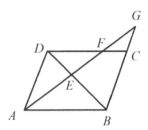

(B) $AE^2 = EF \times EG$

(C) $AE^2 = EG \times FG$

(D) $AE^2 = EF \times AG$

Solution: A.

$\triangle AEB \sim \triangle DEF$ $\Rightarrow$ $\dfrac{EA}{EF} = \dfrac{EB}{ED}$ (1)

$\triangle DAE \sim \triangle BGE$ $\Rightarrow$ $\dfrac{EG}{EA} = \dfrac{EB}{ED}$ (2)

$\dfrac{EA}{EF} = \dfrac{EG}{EA}$ $\Rightarrow$ $AE^2 = EF \times EG$.

  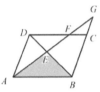 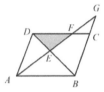

☆**Example 7. (1998 AIME)** Let $ABCD$ be a parallelogram. Extend DA through A to a point P, and let PC meet AB at Q and DB at R. Given that PQ = 735 and QR = 112, find RC.

Solution: 308.

Method 1 (official solution):

The similarity of triangles RBC and RDP implies that

$$\frac{RC}{RP} = \frac{RB}{RD}.$$

The similarity of triangles RBQ and RDC implies that $\dfrac{RB}{RD} = \dfrac{RQ}{RC}$.

Thus $\dfrac{RC}{RP} = \dfrac{RQ}{RC}$, or

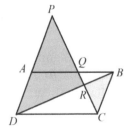 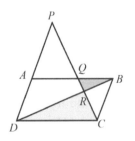

$RC^2 = RQ \times RP = 112 \times 847 = 16 \times 7 \times 7 \times 121$. Hence $RC = 4 \times 7 \times 11 = 308$.

Method 2: (our solution).

$\Delta DRC \sim \Delta BRQ \Rightarrow \quad \dfrac{QR}{RC} = \dfrac{QB}{DC} \quad \Rightarrow \quad \dfrac{112}{RC} = \dfrac{DC - AQ}{DC} = 1 - \dfrac{AQ}{DC}$ (1)

$\Delta APQ \sim \Delta DPC \Rightarrow \quad \dfrac{AQ}{DC} = \dfrac{PQ}{PC} \quad \Rightarrow \quad \dfrac{AQ}{DC} = \dfrac{735}{735 + 112 + RC}$ (2)

Substituting (2) into (1): $\dfrac{112}{RC} = 1 - \dfrac{735}{735 + 112 + RC} \qquad \Rightarrow \qquad RC = 308$.

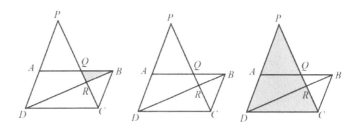

Method 3 (our solution):

$RC^2 = RQ \times RP = 112 \times (735 + 112)$

$RC = \sqrt{112 \times (735 + 112)} = 308$.

Example 8. In parallelogram $ABCD$, point E is the midpoint of AB, and point F is on AD so that $\dfrac{AF}{AD} = \dfrac{1}{3}$. Let G be the point of intersection of AC and FE. Find $\dfrac{AC}{AG}$.

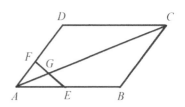

Solution: 005.

Extend FE through E to H and to meet the extension of CB at H.

We know that $AD \parallel CH$. So $\triangle AEF \sim \triangle BEH$ (Figure 1). $\dfrac{AF}{BH} = \dfrac{AE}{EB} \Rightarrow BH = AF$.

So we know that $CH = CB + BH = AD + AF = 4AF$.

We know that $AF \parallel CH$. So $\triangle AGF \sim \triangle CGH$

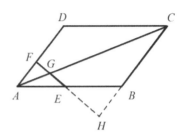

(Figure 2). $\dfrac{AF}{CH} = \dfrac{AG}{GC}$ $\Rightarrow$

$\dfrac{AF}{4AF} = \dfrac{AG}{GC} = \dfrac{1}{4}$ $\Rightarrow$ $\dfrac{GC}{AG} = 4$ $\Rightarrow$

$\dfrac{AC - AG}{AG} = 4 \Rightarrow$ $\dfrac{AC}{AG} - 1 = 4$ $\Rightarrow$ $\dfrac{AC}{AG} = 5$.

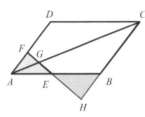   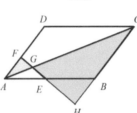

Figure 1   Figure 2

☆ **Example 9.** (2009 AIME) In parallelogram $ABCD$, point M is on AB so that

$\dfrac{AM}{AB} = \dfrac{17}{1000}$, and point N is on AD so that $\dfrac{AN}{AD} = \dfrac{17}{2009}$.

Let P be the point of intersection of AC and MN. Find $\dfrac{AC}{AP}$.

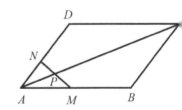

Solution: 177.

Method 1 (official solution):

Let point S be on AC such that NS is parallel to AB. Because $\triangle ASN$ is similar to $\triangle ACD$, $AS/AC = (AP + PS)/AC = AN/AD = 17/2009$.

Because $\triangle PSN$ is similar to $\triangle PAM$, $PS/AP = SN/AM =$

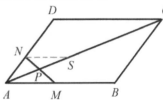

30

$$\frac{\dfrac{17}{2009}CD}{\dfrac{17}{1000}AB} = \frac{1000}{2009}, \text{ and so } \frac{PS}{AP}+1 = \frac{3009}{2009}. \text{ Hence } \frac{\dfrac{17}{2009}AC}{AP} = \frac{3009}{2009}, \text{ and } \frac{AC}{AP} = $$

177.

Method 2 (our solution):
Extend NM through M to E and to meet the extension of CB at E.
We label the line segments as shown in the figure 1.
We know that $AD \text{ // } CE$. So $\triangle AMN \sim \triangle BME$ (Figure

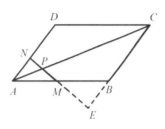

1). $\dfrac{AN}{BE} = \dfrac{AM}{MB} \qquad \Rightarrow \qquad \dfrac{17y}{BE} = \dfrac{17x}{983x} \qquad \Rightarrow$

$\qquad BE = 983y$.

We know that $AN \text{ //} CE$. So $\triangle APN \sim \triangle CPE$ (Figure 2). $\dfrac{AN}{CE} = \dfrac{AP}{PC} \quad \Rightarrow$

$$\frac{17y}{(2009+983)y} = \frac{AP}{AC-AP} \qquad \Rightarrow \qquad \frac{AC}{AP}-1 = \frac{2992}{17} \qquad \Rightarrow$$

$$\frac{AC}{AP} = \frac{2992}{17}+1 = 177.$$

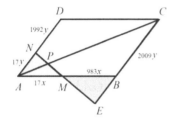

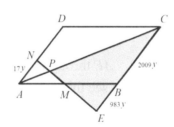

Figure 1   Figure 2

Example 10. In triangle ABC, BM is the median on AC. AE and AF trisect BC and meet BM at G and H, respectively. $BG : GH : HM = x : y : z$. Find the value of $x + y + z$, where x, y, and z are positive integers relatively prime.

Solution: 010.

Method 1:

Connect FM. We see that $FM // AE$ since M is the midpoint of AC and F is the midpoint of EC.

$MF = \dfrac{1}{2} AE = \dfrac{1}{2}(GE + AG) = 2GE$. So $AG = 3GE$ and $MF = \dfrac{2}{3} AG$.

We know that $AG // MF$. So $\triangle AGH \sim \triangle FMH$. $\dfrac{AG}{MF} = \dfrac{GH}{HM} = \dfrac{3}{2}$.

We also know that BG = GM. So $BG : GH : HM = 5 : 3 : 2$. The answer is $5 + 3 + 2 = 10$.

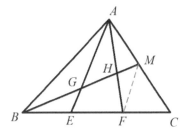
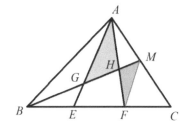

Method 2:

Draw $CP // AF$ and $CQ // AE$ through point C and to meet the extension of BM at P and Q, respectively. We see that $\triangle AGM \equiv \triangle CQM$ ($\angle GAM = \angle QCM$, $AM = MC$, $\angle AMG = \angle CMQ$). So $GM = MQ$.

Similarly we get $HM = MP$.

Let $BG = x$, $GH = y$, $HM = z$.

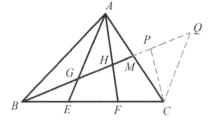

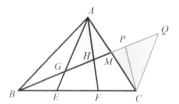 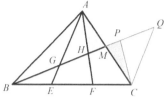 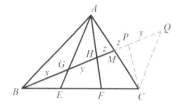

We know that $GE \mathbin{/\mkern-5mu/} CQ$. So $\Delta BEG \sim \Delta BCQ$. $\dfrac{BG}{BQ} = \dfrac{BE}{BC} = \dfrac{1}{3}$.

Therefore $x = y + z$ \hfill (1)

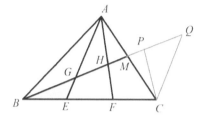 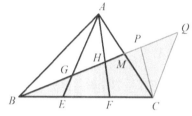

We know that $HF \mathbin{/\mkern-5mu/} PC$. So $\Delta BFH \sim \Delta BCP$. $\dfrac{BH}{BP} = \dfrac{BF}{BC} = \dfrac{2}{3}$ $\quad\Rightarrow\quad \dfrac{x+y}{2x+z} = \dfrac{2}{3}$

.

Therefore $3y = 2z + x$ \hfill (2)

Substituting (1) into (2): $\dfrac{y}{z} = \dfrac{2}{3}$. So $x : y : z = 5 : 3 : 2$. The answer is $5 + 3 + 2 = 10$.

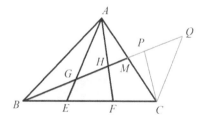 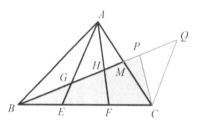

Method 3:

Extend BM to N such that $MN = BM$. Connect AN, CN. $ABCN$ is a parallelogram because the diagonals bisect each other. Thus $AF \parallel BC$. $AN = BC = 3BE$.

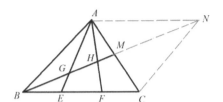

We know that $AN \parallel BC$. So $\triangle BEG \sim \triangle NAG$.

$\dfrac{NG}{BG} = \dfrac{AN}{BE} = 3$. So $NG = 3BG$.

$BN = BG + GN = 4BG$.

$BG = BN/4$.

We know that $AN \parallel BC$. So $\triangle ANH \sim \triangle FBH$. $\dfrac{NH}{BH} = \dfrac{AN}{BF} = \dfrac{3}{2}$. So $NH = 3BH/2$.

$BN = BH + HN = 5BH/2$.

So $BH = 2BN/5$.

Thus $GH = BH - BG = \dfrac{2}{5}BN - \dfrac{1}{4}BN = \dfrac{3}{20}BN$.

$HM = BM - BH = \dfrac{1}{2}BN - \dfrac{2}{5}BN = \dfrac{1}{10}BN$.

$BG : GH : HM = \dfrac{1}{4} : \dfrac{3}{20} : \dfrac{1}{10} = 5 : 3 : 2$

The answer is $5 + 3 + 2 = 10$.

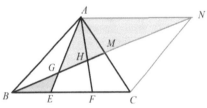
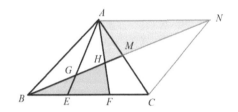

PROBLEMS INVOLVED IN MORE SIMILAR TRIANGLES

Example 11. In triangle ABC, $DE // BC$, BE and CD meet at O. AO meets DE at N, and BC at M, respectively. Show $AN : AM = ON : OM$.

Solution:
We know that $DE // BC$. So we have

$$\triangle ADN \sim \triangle ABM \qquad \Rightarrow \qquad \frac{AN}{AM} = \frac{AD}{AB} \qquad\qquad (1)$$

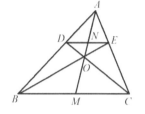 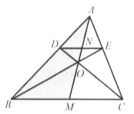

$$\triangle ADE \sim \triangle ABC \qquad \Rightarrow \qquad \frac{AD}{AB} = \frac{DE}{BC} \qquad\qquad (2)$$

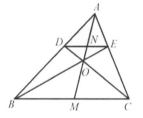 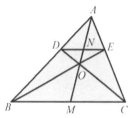

$$\triangle ODE \sim \triangle OCB \qquad \Rightarrow \qquad \frac{DE}{BC} = \frac{OD}{OC} \qquad\qquad (3)$$

$$\triangle ODN \sim \triangle OCM \qquad \Rightarrow \qquad \frac{OD}{OC} = \frac{ON}{OM} \qquad\qquad (4)$$

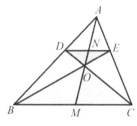 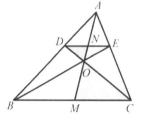

Substituting (2), (3), and (4) into (1): $AN : AM = ON : OM$.

Method 2 (by Kevin Wang)

$$\triangle DOE \sim \triangle COB \qquad \Rightarrow \qquad \frac{DE}{BC} = \frac{NO}{OM} \qquad\qquad (1)$$

$$\triangle ADE \sim \triangle ABC \qquad \Rightarrow \qquad \frac{DE}{BC} = \frac{AN}{AM} \qquad\qquad (2)$$

Thus $\dfrac{DE}{BC} = \dfrac{AN}{AM} = \dfrac{NO}{OM}$.

☆**Example 12.** (2005 AIME II Problem 14) In $\triangle ABC$, $AB = 13$, $BC = 15$, and $CA = 14$. Point D is on BC with $CD = 6$. Point E is on BC such that $\angle BAE = \angle CAD$. Given that $BE = p/q$, where p and q are relatively prime positive integers, find q.

Solution: 463.
Method 1 (official solution):
Let $m\angle BAE = \alpha = m\angle CAD$, and let $\beta = m\angle EAD$. Then

$$\frac{BD}{DC} = \frac{[ABD]}{[ADC]} = \frac{(1/2)AB \cdot AD \sin BAD}{(1/2)AD \cdot AC \sin CAD} = \frac{AB}{AC} \cdot \frac{\sin(\alpha + \beta)}{\sin \alpha}.$$

Similarly,

$$\frac{BE}{EC} = \frac{AB}{AC} \cdot \frac{\sin BAE}{\sin CAE} = \frac{AB}{AC} \cdot \frac{\sin \alpha}{\sin(\alpha + \beta)},$$

and so

$$\frac{BE}{EC} = \frac{AB^2 \cdot DC}{AC^2 \cdot BD}.$$

Substituting the given values yields $BE/EC = (13^2 \cdot 6)/(14^2 \cdot 9) = 169/294$. Therefore $BE = (15 \cdot 169)/(169 + 294) = (3 \cdot 5 \cdot 13^2)/463$. Because none of 3, 5, and 13 divides 463, $q = 463$.

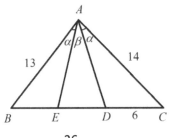

Method 2 (our solution):

Draw $BF \; // \; AC$ to meet the extension of AE at G and AD at F.

We know that $AC \; // BF$. So $\triangle ADC \sim \triangle FDB$ (figure 1). $\dfrac{AC}{BF} = \dfrac{DC}{BD} \quad \Rightarrow$

$$\frac{14}{BF} = \frac{6}{9} \qquad \Rightarrow \qquad BF = \frac{14 \times 9}{6} = 21$$

We know that $\angle BAG = \angle BFA = \alpha$ and $\angle ABG = \angle ABF$ (figures 2 and 3). So

$\triangle ABG \sim \triangle ABF$. $\quad \dfrac{AB}{BF} = \dfrac{BG}{AB} \quad \Rightarrow \quad \dfrac{13}{21} = \dfrac{BG}{13} \Rightarrow \quad BG = \dfrac{169}{21}$

We know that $AC \; // BF$. So $\triangle BGE \sim \triangle CAE$ (figure 4). $\qquad \dfrac{BG}{AC} = \dfrac{BE}{CE}$

$$\Rightarrow \qquad \frac{\dfrac{169}{21}}{14} = \frac{x}{15 - x} \qquad \Rightarrow \qquad x = \frac{2535}{463} .$$

The answer is 463.

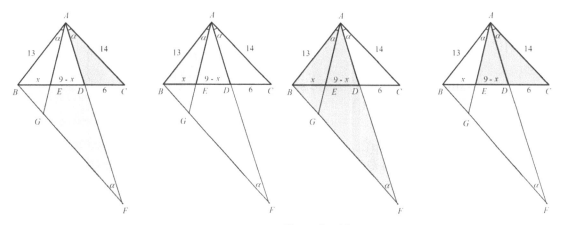

Figure 1   Figures 2 and 3   Figure 4

☆**Example 13.** (2002 AIME II) In triangle ABC, point D is on BC with $CD = 2$ and $DB = 5$, point E is on AC with $CE = 1$ and $EA = 3$, $AB = 8$, and AD and BE intersect at P. Points Q and R lie on AB so that PQ is parallel to CA and PR is parallel to CB. It is given that the ratio of the area of triangle PQR to the area of triangle ABC is m/n, where m and n are relatively prime positive integers. Find $m + n$.

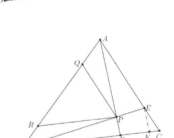

Solution: 901.

Method 1 (official solution):

Draw the line through E parallel to AD, and let K be its intersection with BC.

Because $CD = 2$ and $KC : KD = EC : EA = 1 : 3$, it follows that $KD = 3/2$.

Therefore, $\dfrac{QP}{AE} = \dfrac{BP}{BE} = \dfrac{BD}{BK} = \dfrac{5}{5 + \dfrac{3}{2}} = \dfrac{10}{13}$. Thus

$$\frac{QP}{AC} = \frac{3}{4} \cdot \frac{10}{13} = \frac{15}{26}.$$

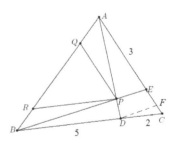

Since triangles PQR and CAB are similar, the ratio of their areas is $(15/26)^2 = 225/676$. Thus $m + n = 901$.

Method 2 (our solution):

Draw the line through D parallel to BE, and let F be its intersection with AC.

Observe that triangles BEC and DFC are similar.

$$\frac{BC}{DC} = \frac{EC}{FC} \quad \Rightarrow \quad \frac{7}{2} = \frac{1}{FC} \quad \Rightarrow \quad FC = \frac{2}{7}$$

So $EF = \dfrac{5}{7}$.

Triangles RPA and BDA are similar.

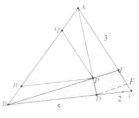 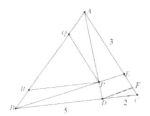

It follows that $\dfrac{RP}{BD} = \dfrac{AP}{AD}$.

Since triangles ADF and APE are similar, so $\dfrac{AE}{AF} = \dfrac{AP}{AD}$.

Thus, $\dfrac{RP}{BD} = \dfrac{AP}{AD} = \dfrac{AE}{AF} = \dfrac{3}{3+\dfrac{5}{7}} = \dfrac{21}{26} \Rightarrow RP = \dfrac{21}{26} \times 5$.

Since triangles PQR and CAB are similar, the ratio of their areas is

$$\dfrac{S_{\triangle PQR}}{S_{\triangle ABC}} = (\dfrac{RP}{BC})^2 = (\dfrac{\dfrac{21}{26}\times 5}{7})^2 = (\dfrac{15}{26})^2 = \dfrac{225}{676}$$

Thus $m + n = 901$.

This is the problem 13 in 2002
AIME II.

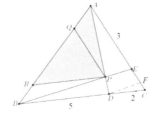 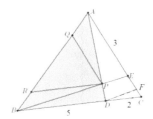

PROBLEMS

Problem 1. In rectangle $ABCD$, BD is the diagonal. $AE \perp BD$. $CF \perp BD$. $BE = 1$ and $EF = 2$. The area of the $ABCD$ can be expressed as $m\sqrt{n}$. What is $100(m + n)$?

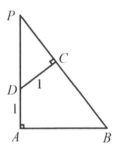

Problem 2. In quadrilateral $ABCD$, $AD = DC = 1$. $\angle DCB = 90°$. The extensions of BC and AD meet at P. Find the smallest value of $AB \times S_{\triangle PAB}$.

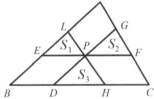

☆**Problem 3.** A point P is chosen in the interior of $\triangle ABC$ so that when lines are drawn through P parallel to the sides of $\triangle ABC$, the resulting smaller triangles, $S_1 = 9$ cm^2, $S_2 = 16$ cm^2, and $S_3 = x$ cm^2 in the figure, respectively. Find the value of x if the area of $\triangle ABC$ is 225 cm^2.

☆**Problem 4:** As shown in the figure, $\triangle ABC$ has the sides $AB = 9$, $BC = 10$, and $CA = 15$. $DE = FG = HI$. $DE \parallel BC$, $FG \parallel AB$, and $HI \parallel AC$. DE, FG, and HI meet at P. Find the product of a and b if $DE = a/b$, where a and b are positive integers relatively prime.

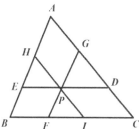

Problem 5: A point P is chosen in the interior of $\triangle ABC$ so that when lines are drawn through P parallel to the sides of $\triangle ABC$. Show that
$$\frac{HF}{BC} + \frac{EL}{CA} + \frac{GD}{AB} = 1.$$

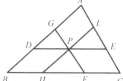

Problem 6. A point P is chosen in the interior of $\triangle ABC$ so that when lines are drawn through P parallel to the sides of $\triangle ABC$ such that $HI = FG = ED$. $AB = 12$, $BC = 8$, and $CA = 6$. The ratios of $AI : IF : FB$ can be expressed in the simplest form of $a : b : c$. a, b, c are positive integers relatively prime. Find the value of $a + b + c$.

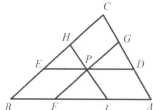

Problem 7. (1998 China Middle School Math Contest) As shown in the figure below, $ABCD$ is a square. A, E, F, and G are in the same line. $AE = 5$ cm and $EF = 3$ cm. Find the sum of a and b if $FG = a/b$, where a and b are positive integers relatively prime.

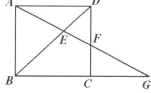

☆**Problem 8.** Let $ABCD$ be a parallelogram. Extend DC through C to a point G, and let AG meet DB at E and BC at F. Show that $AF \times EG = AE \times AG$.

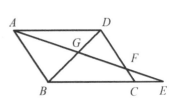

Problem 9. Let $ABCD$ be a parallelogram. Extend BC through C to a point E, and let AE meet BD at G and DC at F. Show that $\dfrac{GD^2}{GB^2} = \dfrac{GF}{GE}$.

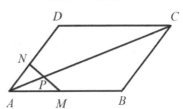

☆**Problem 10.** In parallelogram $ABCD$, point M is on AB so that $\dfrac{AM}{MB} = \dfrac{17}{1000}$, and point N is on AD so that $\dfrac{AN}{ND} = \dfrac{17}{2009}$. Let P be the point of intersection of AC and MN. Find $\dfrac{PC}{PA}$.

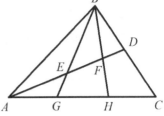

Problem 11. In triangle ABC, AD is the median on BC. BG and BH divide AD into three parts such that $AE : EF : FD = 4:3:1$. $AG : GH : HC = x : y : z$. Find the value of $x + y + z$, where x and y are positive integers relatively prime.

Problem 12. In triangle *AMS, BD // MS, BR* and *DN* meet at *C. AP* goes through *C* and meets *BD* at *O*, and *MS* at *P*, respectively. Show $PM \cdot PN = PS \cdot PR$.

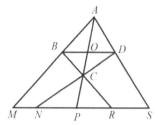

Problem 13. In parallelogram *ABCD, M* is the midpoint of *AB*. The diagonals *AC* and *BD* meet *DM* and *CM* at *G* and *H*, respectively. *GH* meets *AD* at *E* and *BC* at *F*. Show that $EG = GH = HF$.

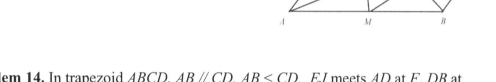

Problem 14. In trapezoid *ABCD, AB // CD, AB < CD*. *EJ* meets *AD* at *F*, *DB* at *G*, *AC* at *H*, *BC* at *I*, respectively, as shown in the figure. Find *DC/AB* if *EF = FG = GH = HI = IJ*.

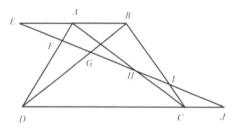

Problem 15. In isosceles triangle *ABC, AD* is the height on *BC*. Draw the height *CE* on *AB*. Draw $DF \perp CE$ and meets *CE* at *F*. Draw $FG \perp AD$ and meets *AD* at *G*.

43

Show that $\dfrac{FG}{AG} = (\dfrac{BD}{AD})^3$.

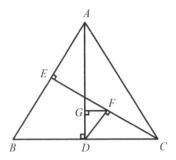

Problem 16. (USAMO) A convex hexagon $ABCDEF$ is inscribed in a circle such that $AB = CD = EF$ and diagonals AD, BE, and CF are concurrent. Let P be the intersection of AD and CE. Prove that

$$\frac{CP}{PE} = \frac{AC^2}{CE^2}.$$

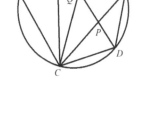

SOLUTIONS

Problem 1. Solution: 700.

We see that $\triangle BAE \cong \triangle CBA$ ($\angle BAE = \angle DCF$, $AB = CD$, $\angle ABE = \angle CDF$).
Thus $BE = FD$. $BD = 1 + 2 + 1 = 4$. $ED = 1 + 2 = 3$.
$\triangle BAE \sim \triangle ADE$ (The height AE divides right triangle ABD into two similar triangles).

$$\frac{AE}{ED} = \frac{BE}{AE} \qquad \Rightarrow \qquad AE = \sqrt{ED \times BE} = \sqrt{3 \times 1} = \sqrt{3}.$$

The area of the $ABCD$ is $BD \times AE = 4\sqrt{3}$. The answer is $10(4 + 3) = 700$.

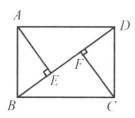   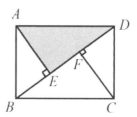

Problem 2. Solution: 004.

Let $PD = x$. $PC = \sqrt{x^2 - 1}$.

We see that $\triangle PCD \sim \triangle PAB$ ($\angle P = \angle P$, $\angle PCD = \angle PAB = 90°$).
Thus $\dfrac{CD}{AB} = \dfrac{PC}{PA}$ $\Rightarrow$ $AB = \dfrac{CD \times PA}{PC} = \dfrac{x+1}{\sqrt{x^2-1}}$

$$AB \times S_{\triangle PAB} = \frac{1}{2} AB^2 \times PA = \frac{(x+1)^3}{2(x^2-1)} = \frac{(x+1)^2}{2(x-1)}.$$

Let $y = \dfrac{(x+1)^2}{2(x-1)}$.

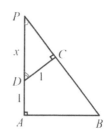   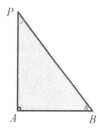

Then we have $2(x-1)y = (x+1)^2 \Rightarrow$
$x^2 + 2(1-y)x + (1+2y) = 0$.
We know that x is real number. So $\Delta = 4(1-y)^2 - 4(1+2y) = 4y(y-4) \geq 0$.
Since $y > 0$, $y \geq 4$. The smallest value of y is 4 (when $x = 3$).

☆**Problem 3.** Solution: 064.

We label the figure as shown.

We know that $EF \parallel BC$ and $LH \parallel AC$. So $\angle LEP = \angle B$.

$\angle ELP = \angle A$. Thus $\triangle LEP \sim \triangle ABC \Rightarrow \dfrac{S_1}{S_{\triangle ABC}} = \dfrac{EP^2}{BC^2}$ (1)

We know that $EBDP$ is a parallelogram, $EP = BD$.

(1) can be written as $\dfrac{\sqrt{S_1}}{\sqrt{S_{\triangle ABC}}} = \dfrac{BD}{BC}$ (2)

Similarly we get: $\dfrac{\sqrt{S_2}}{\sqrt{S_{\triangle ABC}}} = \dfrac{CH}{BC}$ (3)

$\dfrac{\sqrt{S_3}}{\sqrt{S_{\triangle ABC}}} = \dfrac{DH}{BC}$ (4)

(2) + (3) + (4): $\dfrac{\sqrt{S_1}}{\sqrt{S_{\triangle ABC}}} + \dfrac{\sqrt{S_2}}{\sqrt{S_{\triangle ABC}}} + \dfrac{\sqrt{S_3}}{\sqrt{S_{\triangle ABC}}} = \dfrac{BD + CH + DH}{BC} = 1$

$\Rightarrow \sqrt{S_{\triangle ABC}} = \sqrt{S_1} + \sqrt{S_2} + \sqrt{S_3} \Rightarrow S_{\triangle ABC} = (\sqrt{S_1} + \sqrt{S_2} + \sqrt{S_3})^2$

$\Rightarrow 225 = (\sqrt{9} + \sqrt{16} + \sqrt{x})^2 \Rightarrow x = 64$.

☆**Problem 4:** Solution: 180.

Method 1:

Let $DE = m$.

$EH = AB - (BE + AH) = AB - (FP + PG) = 9 - m$.

Similarly $GD = 15 - m$.

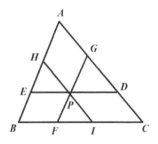

We know that $\triangle DPG \sim \triangle CBA$, so

$DP = \dfrac{BC}{AC} \cdot GD = \dfrac{10}{15}(15 - m) = 10 - \dfrac{2}{3}m$.

We also know that $\triangle PEH \sim \triangle CBA$.

Therefore $PE = \dfrac{BC}{AB} \cdot EH = \dfrac{10}{9}(9 - m) = 10 - \dfrac{10}{9}m$.

Hence $m = DP + PE = 20 - \dfrac{16}{9}m \Rightarrow \quad m = a/b = 36/5.$

$ab = 36 \times 5 = 180.$

Method 2 (by Kevin Wang):
Let FI be x.
$FI : EH : GD = 10 : 9 : 15 = x : (x-1) : (x+5).$

We know that $\Delta HEP \sim \Delta ABC$, so

$EP = \dfrac{BC}{AB} \cdot EH = \dfrac{10}{9}(x-1)$

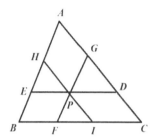

We also know that $\Delta GPD \sim \Delta ABC$.

Therefore $PD = \dfrac{BC}{AB} \cdot GD = \dfrac{10}{15}(x-5) = \dfrac{2}{3}(x-5)$

Hence $EP + PD + FI = 10 \Rightarrow \dfrac{10}{9}(x-1) + \dfrac{2}{3}(x-5) + x = 10.$

Solving for x: $x = 14/5.$
Thus $10 - x = 10 - 14/5 = 36/5.$ The answer is $36 \times 5 = 180.$

Problem 5: Proof:
Since $DE \parallel BC$, $FG \parallel AC$, $LH \parallel AB$, $DP = BH$, $PE = FC$.

We know that $\Delta GDP \sim \Delta BCA$, so $\dfrac{GD}{AB} = \dfrac{DP}{BC}$ (1)

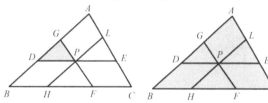

We know that $\Delta PEL \sim \Delta BCA$, so $\dfrac{LE}{AC} = \dfrac{PE}{BC}$ (2)

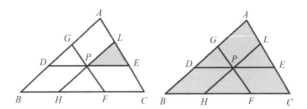

Then we can have: $\dfrac{HF}{BC} + \dfrac{EL}{CA} + \dfrac{GD}{AB} = \dfrac{HF}{BC} + \dfrac{PE}{BC} + \dfrac{DP}{BC} = \dfrac{HF + PE + DP}{BC}$

We see that $DP = BH$. $PE = FC$. So $\dfrac{HF}{BC} + \dfrac{EL}{CA} + \dfrac{GD}{AB} =$

$\dfrac{BH + FC + BF + CH}{BC} = \dfrac{(BH + CH) + (FC + BF)}{BC} = \dfrac{2BC}{BC} = 2\,\dfrac{BC}{BC} = 2\,.$

Problem 6. Solution: 009.

Let $AI = x$, $IF = y$, $FB = z$.

So $x + y + z = 12$ (1)

Since $DE \parallel AB$, $FG \parallel BC$, $IH \parallel AC$, both $AIPD$ and $FBEP$ are parallelograms.

Thus $DP = IA = x$, $PE = FB = z$. $DE = FG = HI = x + z$.

We know that $\triangle AFG \sim \triangle ABC$, so

$\dfrac{FG}{BC} = \dfrac{AF}{AB} \Rightarrow \dfrac{x+z}{8} = \dfrac{x+y}{12}$ (2)

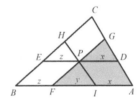

We know that $\triangle BIH \sim \triangle BAC$, so

$\dfrac{HI}{AC} = \dfrac{BI}{AB} \Rightarrow \dfrac{x+z}{6} = \dfrac{y+z}{12}$ (3)

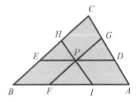

Solving the system of equations (1), (2), and (3): $x = \dfrac{4}{3}$, $y = \dfrac{20}{3}$, $z = 4 = \dfrac{12}{3}$.

Thus $AI : IF : FB = 4 : 20 : 12 = 1 : 5 : 3$.

$a + b + c = 1 + 5 + 3 = 9$.

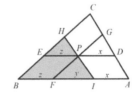

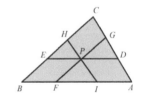

Problem 7. Solution: 019.

We know that $AB//CD$. Thus, $\dfrac{AE}{EF} = \dfrac{BE}{ED}$ (1)

We also know that $CB//AD$. Thus, $\dfrac{BE}{ED} = \dfrac{EG}{AE}$ (2)

From (1) and (2), we get $\dfrac{AE}{EF} = \dfrac{EG}{AE} \Rightarrow EG = \dfrac{AE^2}{EF} = \dfrac{25}{3}$.

So $FG = EG - EF = \dfrac{16}{3}$. The answer is $16 + 3 = 19$.

☆**Problem 8.** Proof:

We know that $AB // DG$. So $\triangle ABE \sim \triangle GDE$

     $\dfrac{AE}{EG} = \dfrac{AB}{DG}$ (1)

We know that $\angle ABC = \angle ADC$ and $\angle BAF = \angle G$. So $\triangle ABF \sim \triangle GDA$

     $\dfrac{AF}{AG} = \dfrac{AB}{DG}$ (2)

From (1) and (2), we get: $\dfrac{AE}{EG} =$

$\dfrac{AF}{AG} \Rightarrow$

     $AF \times EG = AE \times AG$.

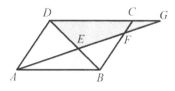 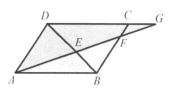

Problem 9. Proof:

We know that $AB // DC$. So $\triangle GDF \sim \triangle GBA.$ $\Rightarrow$ $\dfrac{GD}{GB} = \dfrac{GF}{GA}$ (1)

We know that $AB // AD$. So $\triangle GAD \sim \triangle GBE. \Rightarrow$ $\dfrac{GD}{GB} = \dfrac{GA}{GE}$ (2)

$(1) \times (2)$: $\dfrac{GD^2}{GB^2} = \dfrac{GF}{GE}$.

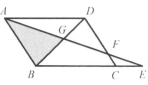 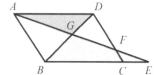

☆**Problem 10.** Solution: 178.

Extend NM through M to E and to meet the extension of CB at E. We label the line segments as shown in the figures.

We know that $AD \parallel CE$. So $\triangle AMN \sim \triangle BME$ (Figure 1). $\dfrac{AN}{BE} = \dfrac{AM}{MB}$ $\Rightarrow$

$$\frac{17y}{BE} = \frac{17x}{1000x} \quad \Rightarrow \quad BE = 1000y.$$

We know that $AN \parallel CE$. So $\triangle APN \sim \triangle CPE$ (Figure 2).

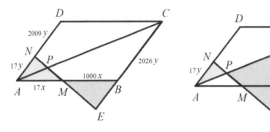

Figure 1   Figure 2

$$\frac{PC}{PA} = \frac{CE}{AN} = \frac{2026y + 1000y}{17y} = 178.$$

Problem 11. Solution: 009.

Extend AD to M and N and connect CM and CN such that $DM = DF$ and $DN = DE$. So $BFCM$ and $BECN$ are parallelograms since the diagonals bisect each other.

Thus $BE \parallel NC$, $BF \parallel MC$.

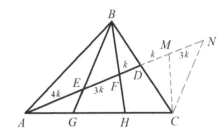

Let $AE = 4k$, $FE = 3k$, and $FD = k$. So $FMN = 3k$, and $DM = k$.

Since $BE \parallel NC$, $\Delta AGE \sim \Delta ACN$. $\dfrac{AE}{AN} = \dfrac{AG}{AC} = \dfrac{4k}{12k} = \dfrac{1}{3}$ $\Rightarrow$

$$AG = \frac{1}{3}AC = \frac{3}{9}AC$$

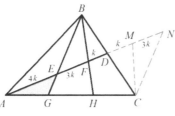
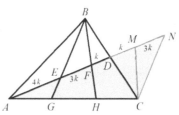

Since $BH \parallel MC$. ΔAHF $\sim \Delta ACM$.

$$\frac{AF}{AM} = \frac{AH}{AC} = \frac{7k}{9k} = \frac{7}{9}$$

$$\Rightarrow \quad AH = \frac{7}{9}AC.$$

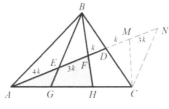
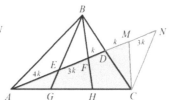

$$GH = AH - AG = \frac{7}{9}AC - \frac{3}{9}AC = \frac{4}{9}AC.$$

$$HC = AC - AH = AC - \frac{7}{9}AC = \frac{2}{9}AC.$$

$AG : GH : HC = 3 : 4 : 2$. The answer is $3 + 4 + 2 = 9$.

Problem 12. Proof:
We know that $BD \parallel MS$. So we have

$$\Delta ABO \sim \Delta AMP \qquad \Rightarrow \qquad \frac{PM}{BO} = \frac{AP}{AO} \qquad (1)$$

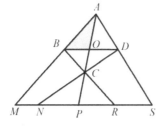
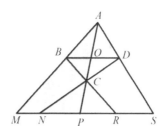

$$\Delta AOD \sim \Delta APS \qquad \Rightarrow \qquad \frac{PS}{OD} = \frac{AP}{AO} \qquad\qquad (2)$$

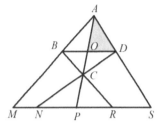 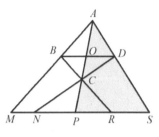

$$\Delta ODC \sim \Delta PNC \qquad \Rightarrow \qquad \frac{PN}{OD} = \frac{PC}{OC} \qquad\qquad (3)$$

$$\Delta OBC \sim \Delta PRC \qquad \Rightarrow \qquad \frac{PR}{OB} = \frac{PC}{OC} \qquad\qquad (4)$$

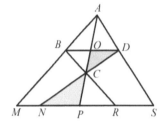 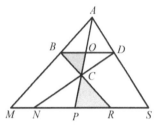

From (1) and (2), we get $\dfrac{PM}{BO} = \dfrac{PS}{OD}$ $\qquad\qquad$ (5)

From (3) and (4), we get $\dfrac{PN}{OD} = \dfrac{PR}{OB}$ $\qquad\qquad$ (6)

(5) × (6): $PM \cdot PN = PS \cdot PR$.

Problem 13. Proof:

We know that $DC \parallel AB$. So we have

$$\Delta AMG \sim \Delta CDG \;\Rightarrow\; \frac{MG}{DG} = \frac{AM}{CD} = \frac{1}{2} \qquad\qquad (1)$$

$$\Delta MBH \sim \Delta CDH \Rightarrow \;\; \frac{MH}{CH} = \frac{MB}{CD} = \frac{1}{2} \qquad\qquad (2)$$

From (1) and (2), we get: $\dfrac{MH}{CH} = \dfrac{MG}{DG} = \dfrac{1}{2}$.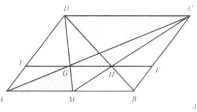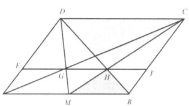

Thus we know that $GH \, // \, DC$, and $EF \, // \, DC \, // \, AB$.

So we know that $\Delta DEG \sim \Delta DAM$.

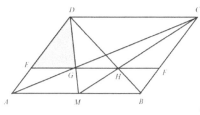 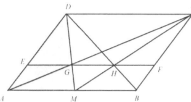

We have $\dfrac{EG}{AM} = \dfrac{DG}{DM} \Rightarrow \quad EG = AM \times \dfrac{DG}{DM} = \dfrac{CD}{2} \times \dfrac{2GM}{2GM + GM} = \dfrac{CD}{3}$.

Similarly we get $HF = \dfrac{CD}{3}$.

$$GH = EF - EG - HF = CD - \dfrac{CD}{3} - \dfrac{CD}{3} = \dfrac{CD}{3} \ .$$

Therefore $EG = GH = HF$.

Problem 14. Proof:

We know that $DC \, // \, AB$. So we have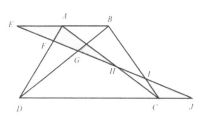

$\Delta EAH \sim \Delta JCH \ \Rightarrow \ \dfrac{EA}{CJ} = \dfrac{EH}{HJ} = \dfrac{3}{2} \quad$ (1)

$\Delta EBI \sim \Delta JCI \ \Rightarrow \ \dfrac{EB}{CJ} = \dfrac{EI}{IJ} = 4 \quad$ (2)

So we get $AB = EB - EA = 4CJ - \dfrac{3}{2}CJ = \dfrac{5}{2}CJ$

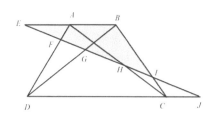

We also have $\Delta EBG \sim \Delta JDG \ \Rightarrow \ \dfrac{EB}{DJ} = \dfrac{EG}{GJ} = \dfrac{2}{3} \quad$ (3)

So we get $\dfrac{2}{3}DJ = 4CJ$ and $DJ = 6CJ$.

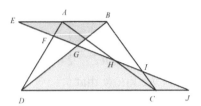

$CD = DJ - CJ = 5CJ.$

We see that $AB = \dfrac{1}{2}CD \Rightarrow \dfrac{DC}{AB} = 2.$

Problem 15. Proof:

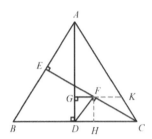

Draw $FH \perp BC$. Extend GF to meet AC at K.
We know that $GF \,/\!/\, BD$. So we have

$$\triangle ABD \sim \triangle DFG \Rightarrow \frac{FG}{GD} = \frac{BD}{AD} \qquad (1)$$

$$\triangle CFI \sim \triangle ADB \Rightarrow \frac{FH}{CH} = \frac{BD}{AD} \qquad (2)$$

$$\triangle AGK \sim \triangle ADB \Rightarrow \frac{KG}{AG} = \frac{BD}{AD} \qquad (3)$$

$$(1) \times (2) \times (3): \frac{FG}{GD} \times \frac{FH}{CH} \times \frac{KG}{AG} = (\frac{BD}{AD})^3 \qquad (4)$$

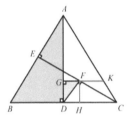 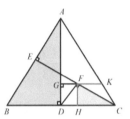 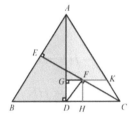

If we connect DK, we see that $\triangle KGD \sim \triangle CFH \Rightarrow \dfrac{KG}{CH} = \dfrac{GD}{FH} \qquad (5)$

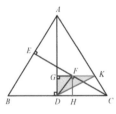 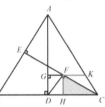

Substituting (5) into (4): $\dfrac{FG}{AG} = (\dfrac{BD}{AD})^3.$

Problem 16. Proof:

Since $CD = EF$, $CF \parallel DE$.

Thus $\triangle CPQ \sim \triangle EPD \Rightarrow \dfrac{CP}{PE} = \dfrac{CQ}{DE}$ (1)

We also know that $\angle QDE = \angle ACE$, $\angle QED = \angle AEC$.

Thus $\triangle QDE \sim \triangle ACE \Rightarrow \dfrac{QD}{DE} = \dfrac{AC}{CE}$ (2)

Similarly, $\triangle CQD \sim \triangle ACE \Rightarrow \dfrac{CQ}{QD} = \dfrac{AC}{CE}$ (3)

$$\frac{CP}{PE} = \frac{CQ}{DE} = \frac{CQ}{DQ} \times \frac{DQ}{DE} = \frac{AC^2}{CE^2}$$

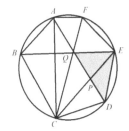 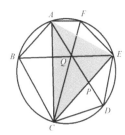 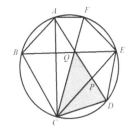 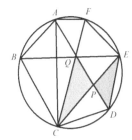

.

BASIC KNOWLEDGE

Below is a list of useful equations to be aware of and know. They can all be derived through expanding or factoring.

Perfect square

$$(x + y + z)^2 = x^2 + y^2 + z^2 + 2xy + 2xz + 2yz$$

$$x^2 + y^2 + z^2 - xy - yz - zx = \frac{1}{2}[(x - y)^2 + (y - z)^2 + (z - x)^2]$$

$$(x + y + z + w)^2 = x^2 + y^2 + z^2 + w^2 + 2xy + 2xz + 2xw + 2yz + 2yw + 2zw$$

$$(a_1 + a_2 + \cdots + a_n)^2$$
$$= a_1^2 + a_2^2 + \cdots + a_n^2 + 2a_1a_2 + 2a_1a_3 + \cdots + 2a_1a_n + 2a_2a_3 + \cdots + 2a_2a_n + \cdots + 2a_{n-1}a_n$$

Difference and sum of two squares

$$x^2 + y^2 = (x + y)^2 - 2xy \qquad\qquad x^2 + y^2 = (x - y)^2 + 2xy$$

$$x^2 - y^2 = (x - y)(x + y)$$

$$x^4 + 4y^4 = (x^2 + 2xy + 2y^2)(x^2 - 2xy + 2y^2)$$

Difference and sum of two cubes

$$x^3 + y^3 = (x + y)(x^2 - xy + y^2)$$

$$x^3 - y^3 = (x - y)(x^2 + xy + y^2)$$

$$x^3 + y^3 + z^3 = (x + y + z)(x^2 + y^2 + z^2 - xy - yz - zx) + 3xyz$$

$$(x + y)^3 = x^3 + 3x^2y + 3xy^2 + y^3 = x^3 + y^3 + 3xy(x + y).$$

$$(x - y)^3 = x^3 - 3x^2y + 3xy^2 - y^3 = x^3 - y^3 - 3xy(x - y).$$

$$x^n - y^n = (x - y)(x^{n-1} + x^{n-2}y + \cdots + y^{n-1}) \text{ for all } n.$$

$$x^n - y^n = (x + y)(x^{n-1} - x^{n-2}y + \ldots - y^{n-1}) \text{ for all even } n.$$

$$x^n + y^n = (x + y)(x^{n-1} - x^{n-2}y + \ldots + y^{n-1}) \text{ for all odd } n.$$

Two Theorems

Theorem 1. Let $a_n = Ax^n + By^n$. Then $a_{n+2} = (x+y)a_{n+1} - xya_n$, n is positive integer.

Proof:

$a_{n+2} = Ax^{n+2} + By^{n+2}$

$= (x+y)(Ax^{n+1} + By^{n+1}) - Ayx^{n+1} - Bxy^{n+1}$

$= (x+y)a_{n+1} - xy(Ax^n + By^n)$

$= (x+y)a_{n+1} - xya_n$

Theorem 2. Let $a_n = Ax^n + By^n + Cz^n$. Then

$a_{n+3} = (x+y+z)a_{n+2} - (xy+yz+zx)a_{n+1} + xyza_n$, n is positive integer.

Proof:

$a_{n+3} = Ax^{n+3} + By^{n+3} + Cz^{n+3}$

$= (x+y+z)(Ax^{n+2} + By^{n+2} + Cz^{n+2}) - Azx^{n+2} - Bxy^{n+2} - Cyz^{n+2} - Cxz^{n+2} - Bzy^{n+2} - Ayx^{n+2}$

$= (x+y+z)a_{n+2} - xy(Ax^{n+1} + By^{n+1}) - yz(By^{n+1} + Cz^{n+1}) - zx(Ax^{n+1} + Cz^{n+1})$

$= (x+y+z)a_{n+2} - (xy+yz+zx)(Ax^{n+1} + By^{n+1} + Cz^{n+1}) + Cxyz^{n+1} + Ayzx^{n+1} + Bzxy^{n+1}$

$= (x+y+z)a_{n+2} - (xy+yz+zx)a_{n+1} + xyza_n$

EXAMPLES

Example 1. Find the value of $a^2 + b^2 + c^2 + d^2$ if
$(a+b+c-d)^2 + (a+b-c+d)^2 + (a-b+c+d)^2 + (-a+b+c+d)^2 = 2016$.

Solution: 504.

$(a+b+c-d)^2 + (a+b-c+d)^2 + (a-b+c+d)^2 + (-a+b+c+d)^2$

$= [(a+b)+(c-d)]^2 + [(a+b)-(c-d)]^2 + [(c+d)+(a-b)]^2 + [(c+d)-(a-b)]^2$

$$= 2(a+b)^2 + 2(c-d)^2 + 2(c+d)^2 + 2(a-b)^2$$
$$= 2[(a+b)^2 + (a-b)^2] + 2[(c+d)^2 + (c-d)^2]$$
$$= 2(2a^2 + 2b^2) + 2(2c^2 + 2d^2)$$
$$= 4(a^2 + b^2 + c^2 + d^2)$$

So we have $4(a^2 + b^2 + c^2 + d^2) = 2016 \quad \Rightarrow \quad a^2 + b^2 + c^2 + d^2 = 2016/4 = 504$.

Example 2. Find the value of $a^2 + b^2 + c^2 - ab - bc - ca$ if $a = 2015x + 2016$, $b = 2015x + 2017$, $c = 2015x + 2018$.

Solution: 003.
$a - b = -1$, $b - c = -1$, $c - a = 2$.

$$a^2 + b^2 + c^2 - ab - bc - ca = \frac{1}{2}[(a-b)^2 + (b-c)^2 + (c-a)^2]$$

$$= \frac{1}{2}[(-1)^2 + (-1)^2 + (2)^2] = 3$$

Example 3. a, b, and c are real numbers. Show that $a = b = c$ if $(a+b+c)^2 = 3(a^2 + b^2 + c^2)$.

Proof:
We know that $(a+b+c)^2 = a^2 + b^2 + c^2 + 2ab + 2bc + 2ca$. So we have
$3(a^2 + b^2 + c^2) = a^2 + b^2 + c^2 + 2ab + 2bc + 2ca$ or
$2a^2 + 2b^2 + 2c^2 - 2ab - 2bc - 2ca = 0$.
By completing the squares: $(a-b)^2 + (b-c)^2 + (c-a)^2 = 0$.
We know that a, b, and c are real numbers. Thus $a - b = 0$, $b - c = 0$, $c - a = 0$.
that is, $a = b = c$.

Example 4. a, b, and c are real numbers such that $a^2 + b^2 + c^2 = 9$. Find the maximum value of $(a-b)^2 + (b-c)^2 + (c-a)^2$.

Solution: 027.

$(a-b)^2 + (b-c)^2 + (c-a)^2 = 2(a^2 + b^2 + c^2) - 2(ab + bc + ca)$

$= 3(a^2 + b^2 + c^2) - [a^2 + b^2 + c^2 + 2(ab + bc + ca)]$

$= 3(a^2 + b^2 + c^2) - (a+b+c)^2 = 27 - (a+b+c)^2 \le 27$.

The maximum value of $(a-b)^2 + (b-c)^2 + (c-a)^2$ is 27 when $a + b + c = 0$.

Example 5. Find the value of a so that $a^2 - b^2 - c^2 + ab = 2019$ and $a^2 + 3b^2 + 3c^2 - 3ab - 2ac - 2bc = -2005$. a, b, and c be positive integers with $a \ge b \ge c$.

Solution: 254.

$$a^2 - b^2 - c^2 + ab = 2019 \qquad (1)$$
$$a^2 + 3b^2 + 3c^2 - 3ab - 2ac - 2bc = -2005 \qquad (2)$$

$$(1) + (2): 2a^2 + 2b^2 + 2c^2 - 2ab - 2bc - 2ac = 14 \qquad (3)$$

(3) can be rearranged to: $(a^2 - 2ab + b^2) + (b^2 - 2bc + c^2) + (a^2 - 2ac + c^2) = 14$.

Or $(a-b)^2 + (b-c)^2 + (a-c)^2 = 14$.

There is one way to express 14 as the sum of three squares of positive integers: $14 = 3^2 + 2^2 + 1^2$.

We know that $a \ge b \ge c$.

Case 1: $a - c = 3$ and $a - b = 2$ and $b - c = 1$.

Case 2: $a - b = 1$ and $b - c = 2$.

We get: $(a, b, c) = (c + 3, c + 1, c)$ or $(a, b, c,) = (c + 3, c + 2, c)$.

In case 1, $2019 = a^2 - c^2 + ab - b^2 = (a-c)(a+c) + (a-b)b = 3(2c+3) + 2(c+1)$

or

$8c + 11 = 2019 \qquad \Rightarrow \qquad c = 251$.

Solving we get $(a,b,c) = (254,252,251)$. The second case has no integer solution. Therefore $a = 254$.

Example 6. Find the last three digits of the greatest positive integer not exceeding $\left(\sqrt{7} + \sqrt{3}\right)^6$.

Solution: 039.

Let $x = \sqrt{7} + \sqrt{3}$ and $y = \sqrt{7} - \sqrt{3}$.

$x + y = (\sqrt{7} + \sqrt{3}) + (\sqrt{7} - \sqrt{3}) = 2\sqrt{7}$.

$xy = (\sqrt{7} + \sqrt{3})(\sqrt{7} - \sqrt{3}) = 7 - 3 = 4$.

$x^2 + y^2 = (x+y)^2 - 2xy = 20$

$x^6 + y^6 = (x^2 + y^2)^3 - 3(x^2 + y^2) \cdot x^2 \cdot y^2 = 7040$.

$(\sqrt{7} + \sqrt{3})^6 + (\sqrt{7} - \sqrt{3})^6 = 7040$.

$(\sqrt{7} + \sqrt{3})^6 = 7040 - (\sqrt{7} - \sqrt{3})^6$.

We know that $0 < \sqrt{7} - \sqrt{3} < 1$, so $0 < \left(\sqrt{7} - \sqrt{3}\right)^6 < 1$.

The greatest positive integer not exceeding $\left(\sqrt{7} + \sqrt{3}\right)^6$ is $7040 - 1 = 7039$. The answer is 039.

☆**Example 7.** Calculate: $\dfrac{(7^4 + 64)(15^4 + 64)(23^4 + 64)(31^4 + 64)(39^4 + 64)}{(3^4 + 64)(11^4 + 64)(19^4 + 64)(27^4 + 64)(35^4 + 64)}$.

Solution: 337.

Method 1:

We know that $x^4 + 4y^4 = (x^2 - 2xy + 2y^2)(x^2 + 2xy + 2y^2)$.

$n^4 + 4 \times 2^4 = (n^2 - 2(n) \times 2 + 2 \times 2^2)(n^2 + 2(n) \times 2 + 2 \times 2^2)$

$= (n^2 - 4n + 8)(n^2 + 4n + 8) = [(n-4)n + 8][n(n+4) + 8]$

$\dfrac{(7^4 + 64)(15^4 + 64)(23^4 + 64)(31^4 + 64)(39^4 + 64)}{(3^4 + 64)(11^4 + 64)(19^4 + 64)(27^4 + 64)(35^4 + 64)}$

$= \dfrac{(3 \times 7 + 8)(7 \times 11 + 8)(11 \times 15 + 8)(15 \times 19 + 8) \cdots (35 \times 39 + 8)(39 \times 43 + 8)}{(-1 \times 3 + 8)(3 \times 7 + 8)(7 \times 11 + 8)(11 \times 15 + 8) \cdots (31 \times 35 + 8)(35 \times 39 + 8)}$

$= \dfrac{39 \times 43 + 8}{-1 \times 3 + 8} = \dfrac{1685}{5} = 337$

Method 2:

We know that $x^4 + 4y^4 = (x^2 - 2xy + 2y^2)(x^2 + 2xy + 2y^2)$.

$n^4 + 4 \times 2^4 = (n^2 - 2(n) \times 2 + 2 \times 2^2)(n^2 + 2(n) \times 2 + 2 \times 2^2)$

$= (n^2 - 4n + 8)(n^2 + 4n + 8) = [(n-2)^2 + 4][(n+2)^2 + 4]$

$\dfrac{(7^4 + 64)(15^4 + 64)(23^4 + 64)(31^4 + 64)(39^4 + 64)}{(3^4 + 64)(11^4 + 64)(19^4 + 64)(27^4 + 64)(35^4 + 64)}$

$= \dfrac{(5^2 + 4)(9^2 + 4)(13^2 + 4)(17^2 + 4) \cdots (37^2 + 4)(41^2 + 4)}{(1^2 + 4)(5^2 + 4)(9^2 + 4)(13^2 + 4) \cdots (33^2 + 4)(37^2 + 4)}$

$= \dfrac{41^2 + 4}{1^2 + 4} = \dfrac{1685}{5} = 337$.

☆**Example 8.** Compute: $\dfrac{(2^4 + \frac{1}{4})(4^4 + \frac{1}{4})(6^4 + \frac{1}{4})(8^4 + \frac{1}{4})(10^4 + \frac{1}{4})}{(1^4 + \frac{1}{4})(3^4 + \frac{1}{4})(5^4 + \frac{1}{4})(7^4 + \frac{1}{4})(9^4 + \frac{1}{4})}$.

Solution: 221.

Method 1:

$$\frac{(2^4 + \frac{1}{4})(4^4 + \frac{1}{4})(6^4 + \frac{1}{4})(8^4 + \frac{1}{4})(10^4 + \frac{1}{4})}{(1^4 + \frac{1}{4})(3^4 + \frac{1}{4})(5^4 + \frac{1}{4})(7^4 + \frac{1}{4})(9^4 + \frac{1}{4})} =$$

$$\frac{(4^4 + 4)(8^4 + 4)(12^4 + 4)(16^4 + 4)(20^4 + 4)}{(2^4 + 4)(6^4 + 4)(10^4 + 4)(14^4 + 4)(18^4 + 4)} \,.$$

We know that

$$n^4 + 4 \times (1)^4 = (n^2 - 2n + 2)(n^2 + 2n + 2) = [(n-1)^2 + 1][(n+1)^2 + 1]\,.$$

So $\dfrac{(4^4 + 4)(8^4 + 4)(12^4 + 4)(16^4 + 4)(20^4 + 4)}{(2^4 + 4)(6^4 + 4)(10^4 + 4)(14^4 + 4)(18^4 + 4)}$

$$= \frac{(3^2 + 1)(5^2 + 1)(7^2 + 1)(9^2 + 1)\cdots(19^2 + 1)(21^2 + 1)}{(1^2 + 1)(3^2 + 1)(5^2 + 1)(7^2 + 1)\cdots(17^2 + 1)(19^2 + 1)}$$

$$= \frac{21^2 + 1}{1^2 + 1} = 221\,.$$

Method 2:

$$n^4 + 4 \times (\frac{1}{2})^4 = [n^2 - 2(n) \times \frac{1}{2} + 2 \times (\frac{1}{2})^2)][n^2 + 2(n) \times \frac{1}{2} + 2 \times (\frac{1}{2})^2)]$$

$$= [(n - \frac{1}{2})^2 + \frac{1}{4})][(n + \frac{1}{2})^2 + \frac{1}{4})]\,.$$

$$\frac{(2^4 + \frac{1}{4})(4^4 + \frac{1}{4})(6^4 + \frac{1}{4})(8^4 + \frac{1}{4})(10^4 + \frac{1}{4})}{(1^4 + \frac{1}{4})(3^4 + \frac{1}{4})(5^4 + \frac{1}{4})(7^4 + \frac{1}{4})(9^4 + \frac{1}{4})} =$$

$$\frac{[(2 - \frac{1}{2})^2 + \frac{1}{4})][(2 + \frac{1}{2})^2 + \frac{1}{4})][(4 - \frac{1}{2})^2 + \frac{1}{4})][(4 + \frac{1}{2})^2 + \frac{1}{4})]\cdots[(10 - \frac{1}{2})^2 + \frac{1}{4})][(10 + \frac{1}{2})^2 +}{[(1 - \frac{1}{2})^2 + \frac{1}{4})][(1 + \frac{1}{2})^2 + \frac{1}{4})][(3 - \frac{1}{2})^2 + \frac{1}{4})][(3 + \frac{1}{2})^2 + \frac{1}{4})]\cdots[(9 - \frac{1}{2})^2 + \frac{1}{4})][(9 + \frac{1}{2})^2 + \frac{1}{4}}$$

$$= \frac{(10 + \frac{1}{2})^2 + \frac{1}{4}}{(1 - \frac{1}{2})^2 + \frac{1}{4}} = \frac{\frac{21^2 + 1}{4}}{\frac{2}{4}} = \frac{442}{2} = 221.$$

General case: $\dfrac{(a_2{}^4 + 4d^4)(a_4{}^4 + 4d^4) \cdots (a_{2n}{}^4 + 4d^4)}{(a_1{}^4 + 4d^4)(a_3{}^4 + 4d^4) \cdots (a_{2n-1}{}^4 + 4d^4)}$,

$a_{2n} - a_{2n-1} = \cdots = a_2 - a_1 = 2d$.

can be simplified into $\dfrac{a_{2n} a_{2n+1} + 2d^2}{a_0 a_1 + 2d^2}$, or $\dfrac{(a_{2n} + d)^2 + d^2}{(a_1 - d)^2 + d^2}$, where $a_0 = a_1 - 2d$.

Example 9. What is the value of $(4 + 2\sqrt{3})^{3/2} - (4 - 2\sqrt{3})^{3/2}$?

Solution: 020.

Method 1:

Let $a = (4 + 2\sqrt{3})^{1/2} = [(\sqrt{3})^2 + 2 \times \sqrt{3} \times 1 + 1^2]^{1/2} = \sqrt{3} + 1$ and

$b = (4 - 2\sqrt{3})^{1/2} = \sqrt{3} - 1$.

We would like to find the value of $(4 + 2\sqrt{3})^{3/2} - (4 - 2\sqrt{3})^{3/2}$

Note that $a^3 - b^3 = (a - b)(a^2 + ab + b^2)$

$= (a - b)(a^2 - 2ab + b^2 + 2ab + ab) = (a - b)[(a - b)^2 + 3ab]$.

$(4 + 2\sqrt{3})^{3/2} - (4 - 2\sqrt{3})^{3/2} = 2[2^2 + 3(\sqrt{3} + 1)(\sqrt{3} - 1)] = 2[4 + 3(3 - 1)] = 20$.

Method 2:

Let $a = (4 + 2\sqrt{3})^{1/2}$ and $b = (4 - 2\sqrt{3})^{1/2}$.

We wish to find $a^3 - b^3 = (a - b)(a^2 + ab + b^2)$.

We can easily calculate the values of the expressions of $a^2 + b^2$ and ab:

$a^2 + b^2 = (4 + 2\sqrt{3}) + (4 - 2\sqrt{3}) = 8$.

$$ab = [(4 + 2\sqrt{3})]^{1/2}[(4 - 2\sqrt{3})]^{1/2} = (4^2 - 2^2 \times 3)^{1/2} = 4^{1/2} = 2.$$

Now we wish to find the value of $a - b$.

We know that $(a - b)^2 = a^2 - 2ab + b^2 = (a^2 + b^2) - 2ab = 8 - 2 \times 2 = 4 \Rightarrow$
$a - b = 2$.

Therefore $a^3 - b^3 = (a - b)(a^2 + ab + b^2) = 2 \times (8 + 2) = 20$.

Example 10. $m = a/b$ is the largest real number z such that
$$x + y + z = 5$$
$$xy + yz + xz = 3$$
and x, y are also real. Find $a + b$ if a and b are positive integers relatively prime.

Solution: 016.

Since $x + y + z = 5$, we have $x + y = 5 - z$.

Squaring both sides gives us $(x + y)^2 = (5 - z)^2$.

Since $xy + yz + xz = 3$, we have $xy = 3 - xz - yz = 3 - z(x + y) = 3 - z(5 - z)$.

$(x - y)^2 = (x + y)^2 - 4xy = (5 - z)^2 - 4[3 - z(5 - z)]$
$= -3z^2 + 10z + 13 = (13 - 3z)(1 + z)$

Since $(x - y)^2 \geq 0$, this means that
$(13 - 3z)(1 + z) \geq 0$.

Solving the inequality gives us
$$-1 \leq z \leq \frac{13}{3}.$$

The largest real number z is $\dfrac{13}{3}$ when $x = y = \dfrac{1}{3}$. The answer is $13 + 3 = 16$.

★**Example 11.** x, y, and z are positive numbers satisfying $xyz = 1$, $x + \dfrac{1}{z} = 10$,

and $y + \dfrac{1}{x} = 17$. If $z + \dfrac{1}{y} = \dfrac{m}{n}$, where m and n are relatively prime positive

integers. Find $m + n$.

Solution: 198.

$$10 \times 17 \times \frac{m}{n} = (x + \frac{1}{z})(y + \frac{1}{x})(z + \frac{1}{y})$$

$$= xyz + x + \frac{1}{z} + y + \frac{1}{x} + z + \frac{1}{y} + \frac{1}{xyz}$$

$$= 1 + 10 + 17 + 1 + \frac{m}{n} = 29 + \frac{m}{n}$$

So we have $10 \times 17 \times \dfrac{m}{n} = 29 + \dfrac{m}{n}$ $\Rightarrow$ $\dfrac{169m}{n} = 29$ $\Rightarrow$ $\dfrac{m}{n} = \dfrac{29}{169}$.

The answer is $29 + 169 = 198$.

★**Example 12.** What is the value of m such that $x^2 - x - 1$ is a factor of $mx^7 + nx^6$ + 1? m and n are integers.

Solution: 008.
Using the quadratic formula, we solve the quadratic equation $x^2 - x - 1 = 0$ to get the roots

$$x_1 = \frac{1 + \sqrt{5}}{2} \text{ and } x_2 = \frac{1 - \sqrt{5}}{2}.$$

We can observe that $x_1 + x_2 = 1$ and $x_1 x_2 = -1$.

Thus, $(x_1 + x_2)^2 = x_1^2 + x_2^2 + 2x_1 x_2 = 1$ and

$$x_1^2 + x_2^2 = 3 \qquad\qquad (1)$$

We know that $x^2 - x - 1$ is a factor of $mx^7 + nx^6 + 1$, so x_1 and x_2 are also the roots of $mx^7 + nx^6 + 1 = 0$.

Therefore we have $mx_1^7 + nx_1^6 = -1$ (2)

and $mx_2^7 + nx_2^6 = -1$ (3)

$(2) \times x_2^6 \implies m x_1^7 x_2^6 + nx_1^6 x_2^6 = -x_2^6 \implies mx_1 (-1)^6 + n(-1)^6 = -x_2^6$

$\implies mx_1 + n = -x_2^6$ (4)

$(3) \times x_1^6: \; mx_2 + n = -x_1^6$ (5)

$(4) - (5): m(x_1 - x_2) = x_1^6 - x_2^6$.

So $m = \dfrac{x_1^6 - x_2^6}{x_1 - x_2} = \dfrac{(x_1^3 - x_2^3)(x_1^3 + x_2^3)}{x_1 - x_2} = \dfrac{(x_1 - x_2)(x_1^2 + x_1 x_2 + x_2^2)(x_1^3 + x_2^3)}{x_1 - x_2}$

$= (x_1^2 + x_1 x_2 + x_2^2)(x_1^3 + x_2^3) = (x_1^2 + x_1 x_2 + x_2^2)(x_1 + x_2)(x_1^2 - x_1 x_2 + x_2^2)$

$= (3 - 1)(1)(3 + 1) = 8$.

★**Example 13.** The real numbers a, b, x, y satisfy $ax + by = 3$, $ax^2 + by^2 = 7$, $ax^3 + by^3 = 16$, $ax^4 + by^4 = 42$. Find $ax^5 + by^5$.

Solution: 020.

By **Theorem 1**, $ax^3 + by^3 = (ax^2 + by^2)(x + y) - (ax + by)xy \implies$

$16 = 7(x + y) - 3xy$ (1)

$ax^4 + by^4 = (ax^3 + by^3)(x + y) - (ax^2 + by^2)xy \implies 42 = 16(x + y) - 7xy$

(2)

Solving (1) and (2) we get: $x + y = -14$ and $xy = -38$.

Therefore $ax^5 + by^5 = (ax^4 + by^4)(x + y) - (ax^3 + by^3)xy =$

$42 \times (-14) - 16 \times (-38) = 20$.

Example 14. For $x < 0$, $x - \dfrac{1}{x} = \sqrt{5}$. $\dfrac{x^{12} - x^{10} + x^6 + x^4 - x^0 + x^{-2}}{x^{12} - x^{10} + x^8 + x^2 - x^0 + x^{-2}} = m/n$, where m

and n are relatively prime positive integers. Find $m + n$.

Solution: 487.

We divided both the numerator and denominator of $\dfrac{x^{12} - x^{10} + x^6 + x^4 - x^0 + x^{-2}}{x^{12} - x^{10} + x^8 + x^2 - x^0 + x^{-2}}$

by x^5:

$$\frac{x^{12} - x^{10} + x^6 + x^4 - x^0 + x^{-2}}{x^{12} - x^{10} + x^8 + x^2 - x^0 + x^{-2}} = \frac{x^7 - x^5 + x^1 + x^{-1} - x^{-5} + x^{-7}}{x^7 - x^5 + x^3 + x^{-3} - x^{-5} + x^{-7}} =$$

$$\frac{(x^7 + x^{-7}) - (x^5 + x^{-5}) + (x^1 + x^{-1})}{(x^7 + x^{-7}) - (x^5 + x^{-5}) + (x^3 + x^{-3})} .$$

Let $a_n = x^n + (\dfrac{1}{x})^n$. We know that $x < 0$, $x - \dfrac{1}{x} = \sqrt{5}$.

So $a_1 = x + \dfrac{1}{x} = -\sqrt{(x - \dfrac{1}{x})^2 + 4x \times \dfrac{1}{x}} = -3$.

$a_2 = x^2 + (\dfrac{1}{x})^2 = (x + \dfrac{1}{x})^2 - 2x \times \dfrac{1}{x} = (-3)^2 - 2 = 7$.

By **Theorem 1**, $a_{n+2} = (x + \dfrac{1}{x})a_{n+1} - x \times \dfrac{1}{x} a_n = (x + \dfrac{1}{x})a_{n+1} + a_n = -3a_{n+1} - a_n$.

$a_3 = -3a_2 - a_1 = -3 \times 7 - (-3) = -18$.

$a_4 = -3a_3 - a_2 = -3 \times (-18) - 7 = 47$

$a_5 = -3a_4 - a_3 = -3 \times 47 - (-18) = -123$

$a_6 = -3a_5 - a_4 = -3 \times (-123) - 47 = 322$

$a_7 = -3a_6 - a_5 = -3 \times 322 - (-123) = -843$.

$$\frac{(x^7 + x^{-7}) - (x^5 + x^{-5}) + (x^1 + x^{-1})}{(x^7 + x^{-7}) - (x^5 + x^{-5}) + (x^3 + x^{-3})} = \frac{a_7 - a_5 + a_1}{a_7 - a_5 + a_3} = \frac{-843 + 123 - 3}{-843 + 123 - 18} = \frac{241}{246} .$$

The answer is $241 + 246 = 487$.

Example 15. x, y, z satisfy $x + y + z = 1$, $x^2 + y^2 + z^2 = 2$, and $x^3 + y^3 + z^3 = 3$. Find $x^5 + y^5 + z^5$.

Solution: 006.

Let $a_n = x^n + y^n + z^n$.

$a_1 = x + y + z = 1$

$a_2 = x^2 + y^2 + z^2 = 2$

$a_3 = x^3 + y^3 + z^3 = 3$

$xy + yz + zx = \dfrac{(x+y+z)^2 - (x^2+y^2+z^2)}{2} = -\dfrac{1}{2}$

$3xyz = x^3 + y^3 + z^3 - (x+y+z)(x^2+y^2+z^2 - xy - yz - zx)$

$= 3xyz = 3 - (1)[(2 - (-\dfrac{1}{2})] = \dfrac{1}{2}$ $\Rightarrow$ $xyz = \dfrac{1}{6}$.

By **Theorem 2**, $a_n = x^n + y^n + z^n$ can be written as

$a_{n+3} = (x+y+z)a_{n+2} - (xy+yz+zx)a_{n+1} + xyz a_n$, n is positive integer.

$a_{n+3} = a_{n+2} + \dfrac{1}{2}a_{n+1} + \dfrac{1}{6}a_n$

So $a_4 = a_3 + \dfrac{1}{2}a_2 + \dfrac{1}{6}a_1 = 3 + \dfrac{1}{2} \times 2 + \dfrac{1}{6} = \dfrac{25}{6}$.

$a_5 = a_4 + \dfrac{1}{2}a_3 + \dfrac{1}{6}a_2 = \dfrac{25}{6} + \dfrac{1}{2} \times 3 + \dfrac{1}{6} \times 2 = 6$.

$x^5 + y^5 + z^5 = 6.$

PROBLEMS

Problem 1.
$$a(b+c-a)^2 + b(c+a-b)^2 + c(a+b-c)^2 + (b+c-a)(c+a-b)(a+b-c) =$$
2016. Find the value of abc.

Problem 2. Find the value of $a^4 + b^4 + c^4 - a^2b^2 - b^2c^2 - c^2a^2$ if $a^2 - b^2 = 1 + \sqrt{2}$, and $b^2 - c^2 = 1 - \sqrt{2}$.

Problem 3. a, b, and c are the lengths of three sides of $\triangle ABC$. Find the area of $\triangle ABC$ if
$$\frac{2a^2}{1+a^2} = b, \quad \frac{2b^2}{1+b^2} = c, \quad \text{and} \quad \frac{2c^2}{1+c^2} = a. \text{ The area of } \triangle ABC \text{ can be expressed as}$$
$\dfrac{\sqrt{m}}{n}$. Find the value of $m + n$ if m and n are positive integers relatively prime.

Problem 4. a, b, and c are real numbers such that $a+b+c=0$, $a^2+b^2+c^2=0.1$. Find the value of $100{,}000(a^4 + b^4 + c^4)$.

Problem 5. $(a+b)(b+c)(c+a) + abc = 66$, a, b, and c are positive integers. Find the value of $a^2 + b^2 + c^2$.

Problem 6. $(ab + bc + ca)(a+b+c) - abc = 140$, a, b, and c are positive integers. Find the value of $a^2 + b^2 + c^2$.

Problem 7. Find the smallest integer greater than $(\sqrt{3} + \sqrt{2})^6$.

Problem 8 Find the last three digits of $\left\lfloor (\sqrt{7} + \sqrt{5})^6 \right\rfloor$.

☆**Problem 9.** Calculate:

$$\frac{(7^4+324)(19^4+324)(31^4+324)(43^4+324)\cdots(103^4+324)}{(1^4+324)(13^4+324)(25^4+324)(37^4+324)\cdots(97^4+324)}.$$

Problem 10. Find the smallest $m+n$ if

$$\frac{(5^4+\frac{1}{4})(7^4+\frac{1}{4})(9^4+\frac{1}{4})(11^4+\frac{1}{4})(13^4+\frac{1}{4})}{(4^4+\frac{1}{4})(6^4+\frac{1}{4})(8^4+\frac{1}{4})(10^4+\frac{1}{4})(12^4+\frac{1}{4})}=\frac{m}{n}.$$

Problem 11. (1990 AIME) Find the value of $(52+6\sqrt{43})^{3/2}-(52-6\sqrt{43})^{3/2}$.

Problem 12. Find x^6+y^6 if $x=\sqrt{5+\sqrt{5}}$ and $y=\sqrt{5-\sqrt{5}}$.

Problem 13. (2010 NC Math Contest) Let x, y, and z be positive real numbers such that $x+y+z=1$ and $xy+yz+xz=1/3$. Find the number of possible values of the expression $\frac{x}{y}+\frac{y}{z}+\frac{z}{x}$.

☆**Problem 14.** Find the last three digits of $m=\dfrac{(x+y)(y+z)(z+x)}{xyz}$ if

$$\frac{x+y}{z}+\frac{y+z}{x}+\frac{z+x}{y}=2015.$$

☆**Problem 15.** x^2-x-1 is a factor of $ax^{17}+bx^{16}+1$ for some integers a and b. Find a

Problem 16. The real numbers a, b, x, y, z satisfy $ax+by+cz=1$, $ax^2+by^2+cz^2=0$, $ax^3+by^3+cz^3=2$, $ax^4+by^4+cz^4=3$, $ax^5+by^5+cz^5=4$, ax^6+by^6+

$cz^6 = 5$. $ax^7 + by^7 + cz^7 = m/n$, where m and n are relatively prime positive integers. Find $m + n$.

Problem 17. The real nonzero numbers a, b, and c satisfy $a + b + c = 0$.

$$\frac{(a^7 + b^7 + c^7)^2}{(a^2 + b^2 + c^2)(a^3 + b^3 + c^3)(a^4 + b^4 + c^4)(a^5 + b^5 + c^5)} = m/n,$$ where m and n are

relatively prime positive integers. Find $m + n$.

Problem 18. (1973 USAMO modified) Find $x^{2015} + y^{2016} + z^{2017}$ if x, y, and z are the real roots of the system of simultaneous equations:

$$\begin{cases} x + y + z = 3, & (1) \\ x^2 + y^2 + z^2 = 3, & (2) \\ x^5 + y^5 + z^5 = 3 & (3) \end{cases}$$

Problem 19. Three numbers x, y, z satisfy $x + y + z = 1$, $x^2 + y^2 + z^2 = 2$, $x^3 + y^3 + z^3 = 3$, and $x^4 + y^4 + z^4 = m/n$, where m and n are relatively prime positive integers. Find $m + n$.

SOLUTIONS

Problem 1. Solution: 504.

Let $b+c-a=x$, $c+a-b=y$, $a+b-c=z$.

So $a=\dfrac{1}{2}(y+z)$, $b=\dfrac{1}{2}(x+z)$, $c=\dfrac{1}{2}(x+y)$.

$a(b+c-a)^2+b(c+a-b)^2+c(a+b-c)^2+(b+c-a)(c+a-b)(a+b-c)$

$=\dfrac{1}{2}[(y+z)x^2+(x+z)y^2+(x+y)z^2+2xyz]$

$=\dfrac{1}{2}[(y+z)x^2+zy(y+z)+xy(y+z)+xz(y+z)]$

$=\dfrac{1}{2}(y+z)[x(x+y)+z(x+y)]$

$=\dfrac{1}{2}(x+y)(y+z)(x+z)=\dfrac{1}{2}(2c)(2a)(2b)=4abc$

So $4abc=2016$ $\Rightarrow$ $abc=2016/4=504$.

Problem 2. Solution: 005

$a^2-c^2=(a^2-b^2)+(b^2-c^2)=2$. $(a^2-c^2)^2=4$.

$(a^2-b^2)^2=3+2\sqrt{2}$, $(b^2-c^2)^2=3-\sqrt{2}$,

$a^4+b^4+c^4-a^2b^2-b^2c^2-c^2a^2=\dfrac{1}{2}[(a^2-b^2)^2+(b^2-c^2)^2+(c^2-a^2)^2]$

$=\dfrac{1}{2}(3+2\sqrt{2}+3-2\sqrt{2}+4)=5$.

Problem 3. Solution: 007.

$\dfrac{2a^2}{1+a^2}=b$ $\qquad\Rightarrow\qquad$ $1+\dfrac{1}{a^2}=\dfrac{2}{b}$ $\qquad\qquad\qquad$ (1)

$\dfrac{2b^2}{1+b^2}=c$ $\qquad\Rightarrow\qquad$ $1+\dfrac{1}{b^2}=\dfrac{2}{c}$ $\qquad\qquad\qquad$ (2)

$$\frac{2c^2}{1+c^2} = a \qquad \Rightarrow \qquad 1+\frac{1}{c^2} = \frac{2}{a} \qquad\qquad (3)$$

$(1) + (2) + (3):\ 1+\dfrac{1}{a^2} + 1+\dfrac{1}{b^2} + 1+\dfrac{1}{c^2} = \dfrac{2}{a}+\dfrac{2}{b}+\dfrac{2}{c} \qquad \Rightarrow$

$(1-\dfrac{1}{a})^2 + (1-\dfrac{1}{b})^2 + (1-\dfrac{1}{c})^2 = 0$.

Thus $a = b = c = 1$. The area of $\triangle ABC$ is $\dfrac{\sqrt{3}}{4}$. The answer is $3 + 4 = 7$.

Problem 4. Solution: 500.

$(a+b+c)^2 = a^2 + b^2 + c^2 + 2ab + 2bc + 2ca \qquad\qquad \Rightarrow$

$\qquad 0 = 0.1 + 2ab + 2bc + 2ca$

$\qquad \Rightarrow \qquad -0.1 = 2ab + 2bc + 2ca \qquad \Rightarrow \qquad ab + bc + ca = -0.05 \ \Rightarrow$

$\qquad (ab + bc + ca)^2 = (-0.05)^2 = 0.05^2$.

We know that $(ab + bc + ca)^2 =$

$a^2b^2 + b^2c^2 + c^2a^2 + 2abc(a+b+c) = a^2b^2 + b^2c^2 + c^2a^2$

$a^4 + b^4 + c^4 = (a^2 + b^2 + c^2)^2 - 2(a^2b^2 + b^2c^2 + c^2a^2) = 0.1^2 - 2\times 0.05^2 = 0.005$.

$100{,}000(a^4 + b^4 + c^4) = 500$.

Problem 5. Solution: 014.

$(a+b)(b+c)(c+a) + abc$

$= (b+c)a^2 + (b+c)^2 a + abc + bc(b+c) = (b+c)a^2 + (b^2 + 3bc + c^2)a + bc(b+c)$

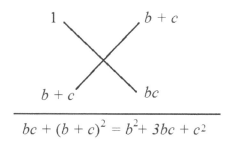

$$bc + (b+c)^2 = b^2 + 3bc + c^2$$

$(a+b)(b+c)(c+a)+abc = (a+b+c)[(b+c)a+bc] = (a+b+c)(ab+bc+ca) = 66.$

So $(a+b+c)(ab+bc+ca) = 66$ $\Rightarrow$ $a+b+c = 6$ and $ab+bc+ca = 11$.

$a^2+b^2+c^2 = (a+b+c)^2 - (2ab+2bc+2ca) = 6^2 - 2\times11 = 36-22 = 14$.

Problem 6. Solution: 026.

$(ab+bc+ca)(a+b+c) - abc$

$= (b+c)a^2 + (b+c)^2 a - abc + bc(b+c) = (b+c)a^2 + (b^2+2bc+c^2)a + bc(b+c)$

$= (b+c)[(a^2 + a(b+c) + bc] = (b+c)(a+b)(c+a)$.

Let $a+b \le b+c \le c+a$.

So $(a+b)(b+c)(c+a) = 140 = 2\times7\times10 = 2\times5\times10 = 4\times5\times7$

Only $(a+b)(b+c)(c+a) = 4\times5\times7$ yields the positive integers solution.

So $a = 3$, $b = 1$, and $c = 4$.

$a^2+b^2+c^2 = 3^2 + 1^2 + 4^2 = 26$.

Problem 7. Solution: 970.

Construct $a_n = (\sqrt{3}+\sqrt{2})^{2n} + (\sqrt{3}-\sqrt{2})^{2n}$

Or $a_n = (5+2\sqrt{6})^n + (5-2\sqrt{6})^n$

$a_{n+2} = [(5+2\sqrt{6}) + (5-2\sqrt{6})]a_{n+1} - (5+2\sqrt{6})(5-2\sqrt{6})a_n = 10a_{n+1} - a_n$

$a_1 = 10$, $a_2 = 98$.

$a_3 = 10\times98 - 10 = 970$.

$a_3 = 10\times98 - 10 = 970 = (5+2\sqrt{6})^3 + (5-2\sqrt{6})^3$

$(5+2\sqrt{6})^3 = 970 - (5-2\sqrt{6})^3$

Since $0 < (5-2\sqrt{6})^3 < 1$

The smallest integer greater than $(5+2\sqrt{6})^3$ is 970.

Problem 8 Solution: 535.

Let $x = \sqrt{7} + \sqrt{5}$ and $y = \sqrt{7} - \sqrt{5}$.

$x + y = (\sqrt{7} + \sqrt{5}) + (\sqrt{7} - \sqrt{5}) = 2\sqrt{7}$.

$xy = (\sqrt{7} + \sqrt{5})(\sqrt{7} - \sqrt{5}) = 7 - 5 = 2$.

$x^2 + y^2 = (x + y)^2 - 2xy = 24$

$x^6 + y^6 = (x^2 + y^2)^3 - 3(x^2 + y^2) \cdot x^2 \cdot y^2 = 13536$.

$(\sqrt{7} + \sqrt{5})^6 + (\sqrt{7} - \sqrt{5})^6 = 13536$.

$(\sqrt{7} + \sqrt{5})^6 = 13536 - (\sqrt{7} - \sqrt{5})^6$.

We know that $0 < \sqrt{7} - \sqrt{5} < 1$. So $0 < \left(\sqrt{7} - \sqrt{5}\right)^6 < 1$.

The greatest positive integer not exceeding $\left(\sqrt{7} + \sqrt{5}\right)^6$ is $13536 - 1 = 13535$.

☆**Problem 9.** Solution: 865.

We know that $x^4 + 4y^4 = (x^2 - 2xy + 2y^2)(x^2 + 2xy + 2y^2)$.

$n^4 + 4 \times 3^4 = (n^2 - 2 \times n \times 3 + 2 \times 3^2)(n^2 + 2 \times n \times 3 + 2 \times 3^2)$

$= (n^2 + 6n + 18)(n^2 - 6n + 18) = [(n-6)n + 18][n(n+6) + 18]$

$\dfrac{(7^4 + 324)(19^4 + 324)(31^4 + 324)(43^4 + 324) \cdots (103^4 + 324)}{(1^4 + 324)(13^4 + 324)(25^4 + 324)(37^4 + 324) \cdots (97^4 + 324)}$

$=$

$\dfrac{(1 \times 7 + 18)(7 \times 13 + 18)(13 \times 19 + 18)(19 \times 25 + 18) \cdots (97 \times 103 + 18)(103 \times 109 + 18)}{(-5 \times 1 + 18)(1 \times 7 + 18)(7 \times 13 + 18)(13 \times 19 + 18) \cdots (91 \times 97 + 18)(97 \times 103 + 18)}$

$= \dfrac{103 \times 109 + 18}{-5 \times 1 + 18} = \dfrac{11245}{13} = 865$.

Problem 10. Solution: 078.

$n^4 + 4 \times (\dfrac{1}{2})^4 = [n^2 - 2(n) \times \dfrac{1}{2} + 2 \times (\dfrac{1}{2})^2)][n^2 + 2(n) \times \dfrac{1}{2} + 2 \times (\dfrac{1}{2})^2)]$

$= [(n - \dfrac{1}{2})^2 + \dfrac{1}{4})][(n + \dfrac{1}{2})^2 + \dfrac{1}{4})]$.

$$\frac{(5^4+\frac{1}{4})(7^4+\frac{1}{4})(9^4+\frac{1}{4})(11^4+\frac{1}{4})(13^4+\frac{1}{4})}{(4^4+\frac{1}{4})(6^4+\frac{1}{4})(8^4+\frac{1}{4})(10^4+\frac{1}{4})(12^4+\frac{1}{4})}=$$

$$\frac{[(5-\frac{1}{2})^2+\frac{1}{4}][(5+\frac{1}{2})^2+\frac{1}{4}][7-\frac{1}{2})^2+\frac{1}{4}][(7+\frac{1}{2})^2+\frac{1}{4}]\cdots[(13-\frac{1}{2})^2+\frac{1}{4}][(13+\frac{1}{2})^2+\frac{1}{4}}{[(4-\frac{1}{2})^2+\frac{1}{4}][(4+\frac{1}{2})^2+\frac{1}{4}][(6-\frac{1}{2})^2+\frac{1}{4}][(6+\frac{1}{2})^2+\frac{1}{4}]\cdots[(12-\frac{1}{2})^2+\frac{1}{4}][(12+\frac{1}{2})^2+\frac{1}{4}}$$

$$=\frac{(13+\frac{1}{2})^2+\frac{1}{4}}{(4-\frac{1}{2})^2+\frac{1}{4}}=\frac{\frac{27^2+1}{4}}{\frac{50}{4}}=\frac{730}{50}=\frac{73}{5}.\text{ So }m+n=73+5=78.$$

Problem 11. Solution: 828.

Method 1:

Let $a=(52+6\sqrt{43})^{1/2}=[(\sqrt{43})^2+2\times\sqrt{43}\times3+3^2]^{1/2}=\sqrt{43}+3$ and

$b=(52-6\sqrt{43})^{1/2}=\sqrt{43}-3$.

We would like to find the value of $(52+6\sqrt{43})^{3/2}-(52-6\sqrt{43})^{3/2}$.

Note that $a^3-b^3=(a-b)(a^2+ab+b^2)=(a-b)(a^2-2ab+b^2+2ab+ab)$

$=(a-b)[(a-b)^2+3ab]$

$(52+6\sqrt{43})^{3/2}-(52-6\sqrt{43})^{3/2}$

$=6[6^2+3(\sqrt{43}+3)(\sqrt{43}-3)]=6[36+3(43-9)]=828$.

Method 2:

Let $a=(52+6\sqrt{43})^{1/2}$ and $b=(52-6\sqrt{43})^{1/2}$.

We wish to find $a^3-b^3=(a-b)(a^2+ab+b^2)$.

We can easily calculate the values of the expressions of a^2+b^2 and ab:

$a^2+b^2=(52+6\sqrt{43})+(52-6\sqrt{43})=104$.

$$ab = [(52 + 6\sqrt{43})]^{1/2}[(52 - 6\sqrt{43})]^{1/2} = (52^2 - 6^2 \times 43)^{1/2} = 1156^{1/2} = 34.$$

Now we wish to find the value of $a - b$.

We know that $(a - b)^2 = a^2 - 2ab + b^2 = (a^2 + b^2) - 2ab = 104 - 2 \times 34 = 36 \implies$

$a - b = 6$.

Therefore $a^3 - b^3 = (a - b)(a^2 + ab + b^2) = 6 \times (104 + 34) = 828$.

Problem 12. Solution: 400.

Since $x = \sqrt{5 + \sqrt{5}}$ and $y = \sqrt{5 - \sqrt{5}}$, $x^2 \cdot y^2 = (5 + \sqrt{5})(5 - \sqrt{5}) = 25 - 5 = 20$.

$x^2 + y^2 = (5 + \sqrt{5}) + (5 - \sqrt{5}) = 10$

$x^6 + y^6 = (x^2 + y^2)^3 - 3(x^2 + y^2) \cdot x^2 \cdot y^2 = 10^3 - 3 \times 10 \times 20 = 400$

(If you are confused about the equation above, expand out

$(x^2 + y^2)^3 - 3(x^2 + y^2) \cdot x^2 \cdot y^2$)

Problem 13. Solution: 001.

Since $1 = (x + y + z)^2 = x^2 + y^2 + z^2 + 2(xy + yz + xz) = x^2 + y^2 + z^2 + 2/3$, we get

$x^2 + y^2 + z^2 = 1/3$. Then $x^2 + y^2 + z^2 - xy - yz - xz = 0$.

We know that $x^2 + y^2 + z^2 - xy - yz - zx = \dfrac{1}{2}[(x - y)^2 + (y - z)^2 + (z - x)^2]$.

Therefore $\dfrac{1}{2}[(x - y)^2 + (y - z)^2 + (z - x)^2] = 0$.

Since x, y, and z are positive real numbers, we have $x = y = z$, which implies that

$\dfrac{x}{y} + \dfrac{y}{z} + \dfrac{z}{x} = 3$. 3 is the only value for $\dfrac{x}{y} + \dfrac{y}{z} + \dfrac{z}{x}$.

☆**Problem 14.** Solution: 017.

$$\frac{(x + y)(y + z)(z + x)}{xyz} = \frac{(x^2 y + xy^2) + (x^2 z + xz^2) + (y^2 z + yz^2) + 2xyz}{xyz}$$

$$= \frac{xy(x + y) + xz(x + z) + yz(y + z) + 2xyz}{xyz}$$

$$= \frac{x+y}{z} + \frac{y+z}{x} + \frac{z+x}{y} + 2 = 2015 + 2 = 2017.$$

☆**Problem 15.** Solution: 987.

Using the quadratic formula, we see that the quadratic equation $x^2 - x - 1 = 0$ has

the solutions: $p = \dfrac{1+\sqrt{5}}{2}$ and $q = \dfrac{1-\sqrt{5}}{2}$.

We can observe that $p + q = 1$ and $pq = -1$.

Since $x^2 - x - 1$ is a factor of $ax^{17} + bx^{16} + 1$, p and q are also the roots of $ax^{17} + bx^{16} + 1 = 0$.

Therefore we have $ap^{17} + bp^{16} = -1$ (1)

and $aq^{17} + bq^{16} = -1$ (2)

$(1) \times q^{16} \Rightarrow ap^{17}q^{16} + bp^{16}q^{16} = -q^{16} \Rightarrow ap(-1)^{16} + b(-1)^{16} = -q^{16}$

$\Rightarrow \quad ap + b = -q^{16}$ (3)

$(2) \times p^{16}$: $aq + b = -p^{16}$ (4)

$(3) - (4)$: $a(p - q) = p^{16} - q^{16}$.

So

$$a = \frac{p^{16} - q^{16}}{p - q} = \frac{(p^8 + q^8)(p^8 - q^8)}{p - q} = \frac{(p^8 + q^8)(p^4 + q^4)(p^4 - q^4)}{p - q}$$

$$= \frac{(p^8 + q^8)(p^4 + q^4)(p^2 + q^2)(p^2 - q^2)}{p - q} = \frac{(p^8 + q^8)(p^4 + q^4)(p^2 + q^2)(p + q)(p - q)}{p - q}.$$

$$= (p^8 + q^8)(p^4 + q^4)(p^2 + q^2)(p + q)$$

Since $(p + q)^2 = p^2 + q^2 + 2pq$, we can calculate that:

$p^2 + q^2 = (p+q)^2 - 2pq = 1 + 2 = 3$.

Similarly, $p^4 + q^4 = (p^2 + q^2)^2 - 2(pq)^2 = 9 - 2 = 7$

and $p^8 + q^8 = (p^4 + q^4)^2 - 2(pq)^4 = 49 - 2 = 47$.

Therefore $a = 47 \times 7 \times 3 \times 1 = 987$.

Problem 16. Solution: 064.

By **Theorem 2**, $a_n = Ax^n + By^n + Cz^n$ can be written as

$a_{n+3} = (x+y+z)a_{n+2} - (xy+yz+zx)a_{n+1} + xyza_n$, n is positive integer.

Let $A_1 = x+y+z$, $A_2 = -(xy+yz+zx)$, and $A_3 = xyz$.

Then we have $a_{n+3} = A_1 a_{n+2} + A_2 a_{n+1} + A_3 a_n$ (1)

We know that $a_1 = 1$, $a_2 = 0$, $a_3 = 2$, $a_4 = 3$, $a_5 = 4$, $a_6 = 5$.

Substituting these values into (1):

$2A_1 + 0 \times A_2 + A_3 = 3$ (2)

$3A_1 + 2 \times A_2 + 0 \times A_3 = 4$ (3)

$4A_1 + 3A_2 + 2A_3 = 5$ (4)

Solving the system of equations (2), (3), and (4):

$A_1 = \dfrac{14}{9}$, $A_2 = -\dfrac{1}{3}$, $A_3 = -\dfrac{1}{9}$.

Thus we get $a_{n+3} = \dfrac{14}{9} a_{n+2} - \dfrac{1}{3} a_{n+1} - \dfrac{1}{9} a_n$.

When $n = 4$, we get $a_7 = \dfrac{14}{9} a_6 - \dfrac{1}{3} a_5 - \dfrac{1}{9} a_4 = \dfrac{14}{9} \times 5 - \dfrac{1}{3} \times 4 - \dfrac{1}{9} \times 3 = \dfrac{55}{9}$.

The answer is $55 + 9 = 64$,

Problem 17. Solution: 109.

Let $a_n = a^n + b^n + c^n$.

$a_1 = a+b+c = 0$

$a_2 = a^2 + b^2 + c^2 = (a+b+c)^2 - 2(ab+bc+ca) = -2(ab+bc+ca)$.

$a_3 = a^3 + b^3 + c^3 = (a+b+c)(a^2+b^2+c^2-bc-ca-ab) + 3abc = 3abc$

By **Theorem 2**, $a_n = a^n + b^n + c^n$ can be written as

$a_{n+3} = (a+b+c)a_{n+2} - (ab+bc+ca)a_{n+1} + abca_n$

$= -(ab+bc+ca)a_{n+1} + abca_n = \dfrac{1}{2} a_2 a_{n+1} + \dfrac{1}{3} a_3 a_n$

Then we have

$$a_4 = \frac{1}{2}a_2a_2 + \frac{1}{3}a_3a_1 = \frac{1}{2}a_2^{\,2}$$

$$a_5 = \frac{1}{2}a_2a_3 + \frac{1}{3}a_3a_2 = \frac{5}{6}a_2a_3$$

$$a_7 = \frac{1}{2}a_2a_5 + \frac{1}{3}a_3a_4 = \frac{1}{2}a_2 \times \frac{5}{6}a_2a_3 + \frac{1}{3}a_3 \times \frac{1}{2}a_2^{\,2} = \frac{7}{12}a_2^{\,2}a_3.$$

Therefore $\dfrac{(a^7 + b^7 + c^7)^2}{(a^2 + b^2 + c^2)(a^3 + b^3 + c^3)(a^4 + b^4 + c^4)(a^5 + b^5 + c^5)}$

$$= \frac{(a_7)^2}{a_2a_3a_4a_5} = \frac{(\frac{7}{12}a_2^{\,2}a_3)^2}{a_2a_3 \cdot \frac{1}{2}a_2^{\,2} \cdot \frac{5}{6}a_2a_3} = \frac{49}{60}.$$

The answer is $49 + 60 = 109$.

Problem 18. Solution: 003.

$(2) - (1) \times 2$:

$x^2 + y^2 + z^2 - 2x - 2y - 2z = -3$

Completing the square: $(x-1)^2 + (y-1)^2 + (z-1)^2 = 0$

$\therefore\ x = 1,\ y = 1,\ z = 1.\ x^{2015} + y^{2016} + z^{2017} = 3.$

Problem 19. Solution: 031.

$$xy + yz + xz = \frac{1}{2}[(x+y+z)^2 - (x^2 + y^2 + z^2)] = \frac{1}{2}(1^2 - 2) = -\frac{1}{2}.$$

$$x^4 + y^4 + z^4 = (x^2 + y^2 + z^2)^2 - 2(x^2y^2 + y^2z^2 + z^2x^2)$$

$$= 2^2 - 2[(xy + yz + zx)^2 - 2xyz(x + y + z)]$$

$$= 4 - 2[(-\frac{1}{2})^2 - 2xyz] = \frac{7}{2} + 4xyz$$

We also know that $x^3 + y^3 + z^3 = (x+y+z)(x^2 + y^2 + z^2 - xy - yz - zx) + 3xyz$.

So $3 - 3xyz = 2 - (-\dfrac{1}{2})$ $\Rightarrow xyz = \dfrac{1}{6}$.

Thus $x^4 + y^4 + z^4 = \dfrac{7}{2} + 4xyz = \dfrac{7}{2} + 4 \times \dfrac{1}{6} = \dfrac{25}{6}$.

The answer is $25 + 6 = 31$.

1. SYSTEM OF LINEAR EQUATIONS

A group (two or more) of equations is called a system of equations. The solutions of a system of equations should satisfy all the equations.

A system of two equations is as follows:

$$\begin{cases} a_1x + b_1y = c_1 \\ a_2x + b_2y = c_2 \end{cases} \qquad\qquad (1) \\ \qquad\qquad (2)$$

Case I: When $\dfrac{a_1}{a_2} \neq \dfrac{b_1}{b_2}$, the system of equations has one solution:

Case II: When $\dfrac{a_1}{a_2} = \dfrac{b_1}{b_2} = \dfrac{c_1}{c_2}$, the system of equations has infinitely many solutions.

Case III: When $\dfrac{a_1}{a_2} = \dfrac{b_1}{b_2} \neq \dfrac{c_1}{c_2}$, the system of equations has no solution.

The two commonly used methods to solve a system of equations are substitution and elimination methods.

Example 1. Find $3x + 2y + 6z$ if x, y, and z satisfy the system of equations

$$\begin{cases} (x+y):(y+z):(z+x) = 3:4:5 \\ 7x + 3y - 5z = 4 \end{cases} \qquad\qquad (1) \\ \qquad\qquad (2)$$

Solution: 052.

Let $x + y = 3k$ $\qquad\qquad\qquad\qquad\qquad\qquad (3)$

$\qquad\quad y + z = 4k$ $\qquad\qquad\qquad\qquad\qquad\qquad (4)$

$\qquad\quad z + x = 5k$ $\qquad\qquad\qquad\qquad\qquad\qquad (5)$

$k \neq 0$.

(3) + (4) + (5): $2(x + y + z) = 12k \quad \Rightarrow \quad x + y + z = 6k$ $\qquad (6)$

(6) – (3), (6) – (4), and (6) – (5), we get $x = 2k$, $y = k$, and $z = 3k$. Substituting these values into (2): $14k + 3k - 15k = 4 \quad \Rightarrow \quad k = 2$

$3x + 2y + 6z = 6k + 2k + 19k = 12 + 4 + 36 = 52$

☆ **Example 2.** Find $3x + 4y + 5z$ if x, y, z, u, and v satisfy the system of equations

$$\begin{cases} 2x + y + z + u + v = 16 & (1) \\ x + 2y + z + u + v = 17 & (2) \\ x + y + 2z + u + v = 18 & (3) \\ x + y + z + 2u + v = 19 & (4) \\ x + y + z + u + 2v = 20 & (5) \end{cases}$$

Solution: 026.

(1) + (2) + (3) + (4) + (5): $6(x + y + z + u + v) = 90 \implies x + y + z + u + v = 15$
      (6)

(1) − (6): $x = 1$.
(2) − (6): $y = 2$.
(3) − (6): $z = 3$.
$3x + 4y + 5z = 3 + 8 + 15 = 26$.

☆**Example 3.** Find $16 x_1 + 25 x_2 + 36 x_3 + 49 x_4 + 64 x_5 + 81 x_6 + 100 x_7$ given that:

$x_1 + 4 x_2 + 9 x_3 + 16 x_4 + 25 x_5 + 36 x_6 + 49 x_7 = 1$ (1)
$4 x_1 + 9 x_2 + 16 x_3 + 25 x_4 + 36 x_5 + 49 x_6 + 64 x_7 = 12$ (2)
$9 x_1 + 16 x_2 + 25 x_3 + 36 x_4 + 49 x_5 + 64 x_6 + 81 x_7 = 123$ (3)

Solution: 334.

Method 1:
$3 \times (2)$: $12 x_1 + 27 x_2 + 48 x_3 + 75 x_4 + 108 x_5 + 147 x_6 + 192 x_7 = 36$ (4)
$3 \times (3)$: $27 x_1 + 48 x_2 + 75 x_3 + 108 x_4 + 147 x_5 + 192 x_6 + 243 x_7 = 369$ (5)
$(5) - (4)$: $15 x_1 + 21 x_2 + 27 x_3 + 33 x_4 + 39 x_5 + 45 x_6 + 51 x_7 = 333$ (6)
$(6) + (1)$: $16 x_1 + 25 x_2 + 36 x_3 + 49 x_4 + 64 x_5 + 81 x_6 + 100 x_7 = 334$

Method 2 (by Anthony Cheng):

$(2) - (1)$: $3x_1 + 5x_2 + 7x_3 + 9x_4 + 11x_5 + 13x_6 + 15x_7 = 11$ (4)

$(3) - (2)$: $5x_1 + 7x_2 + 9x_3 + 11x_4 + 13x_5 + 15x_6 + 17x_7 = 111$ (5)

$(5) - (4)$: $2x_1 + 2x_2 + 2x_3 + 2x_4 + 2x_5 + 2x_6 + 2x_7 = 100$ (6)

$(5) + (6)$: $7x_1 + 9x_2 + 11x_3 + 13x_4 + 15x_5 + 17x_6 + 19x_7 = 211$ (7)

$(7) + (3)$: $16x_1 + 25x_2 + 36x_3 + 49x_4 + 64x_5 + 81x_6 + 100x_7 = 334$

Example 4. Find $\sum\limits_{100}^{i=1} x_i^2$ if $x_1, x_2, x_3, x_4, \cdots, x_{100}$ satisfy the system of equations

$$\begin{cases} x_1 + 2x_2 + 2x_3 + 2x_4 + 2x_5 + \cdots + 2x_{100} = 1 \\ (1) \\ x_1 + 3x_2 + 4x_3 + 4x_4 + 4x_5 + \cdots + 4x_{100} = 2 \\ (2) \\ x_1 + 3x_2 + 5x_3 + 6x_4 + 6x_5 + \cdots + 6x_{100} = 3 \\ (3) \\ x_1 + 3x_2 + 5x_3 + 7x_4 + 8x_5 + \cdots + 8x_{100} = 4 \\ (4) \\ \cdots \quad \cdots \quad \cdots \quad \cdots \quad \cdots \\ x_1 + 3x_2 + 5x_3 + 7x_4 + 9x_5 + \cdots + 199x_{100} = 100 \\ (100) \end{cases}$$

Solution: 100.

$(2) - (1)$, $(3) - (1)$, ... $(100) - (1)$, we get

$$\begin{cases} x_2 + 2x_3 + 2x_4 + 2x_5 + \cdots + 2x_{100} = 1 \\ x_2 + 3x_3 + 4x_4 + 4x_5 + \cdots + 4x_{100} = 2 \\ x_2 + 3x_3 + 5x_4 + 6x_5 + \cdots + 6x_{100} = 3 \\ \cdots \quad \cdots \quad \cdots \quad \cdots \\ x_2 + 3x_3 + 5x_4 + 7x_5 + \cdots + 197x_{100} = 99 \end{cases}$$

We repeat the same procedure and we will get 100 systems of equations. We then create a new system of equations by using the first equation in each of the 100 systems of equations:

$$\begin{cases} x_1 + 2x_2 + 2x_3 + 2x_4 + 2x_5 + \cdots + 2x_{100} = 1 \\ x_2 + 2x_3 + 2x_4 + 2x_5 + \cdots + 2x_{100} = 1 \\ x_3 + 2x_4 + 2x_5 + \cdots + 2x_{100} = 1 \\ \cdots \quad\quad \cdots \quad\quad \cdots \quad\quad \cdots \\ x_{99} + 2x_{100} = 1 \\ x_{100} = 1 \end{cases}$$

So we get the solutions: $x_1 = -1$, $x_2 = 1$, $x_3 = -1$, $x_4 = 1$,.. , $x_{99} = -1$, $x_{100} = 1$.

$$\sum_{100}^{i=1} x_i^2 = 100.$$

2. SOME SKILLS FOR SOLVING NONLINEAR EQUATIONS

2.1. Method of Constructing the Variance

Let $\overline{x}$ be the mean of $x_1, x_2, x_3, \ldots, x_n$.
The variance is:

$$s^2 = \frac{1}{n}[(x_1 - \overline{x})^2 + (x_2 - \overline{x})^2 + \cdots + (x_n - \overline{x})^2]$$

$$= \frac{1}{n}[(x_1^2 + x_2^2 + \cdots + x_n^2) - \frac{1}{n}(x_1 + x_2 + \cdots + x_n)^2].$$

It is clear that $s \geq 0$ (with equality if and only if $x_1 = x_2 = x_3 = \ldots = x_n = \overline{x}$).

Example 5: Find $100x$ if x and y are real numbers satisfying

$$\begin{cases} x + y = 2, \\ xy - z^2 = 1 \end{cases}$$

Solution: 100.

Rewrite the given equations as

$$\begin{cases} x + y = 2, \\ xy = 1 + z^2 \end{cases}$$

The variance is of x and y is:

$$s^2 = \frac{1}{2}[(x^2 + y^2) - \frac{1}{2}(x+y)^2] = \frac{1}{2}[\frac{1}{2}(x+y)^2 - 2xy] = \frac{1}{2}[2 - 2(1+z^2)] \geq 0 \Rightarrow z^2 \leq 0.$$

Thus, z must be 0.

Substituting $z = 0$ into the given equations, we find: $x = 1$, $y = 1$.

The solutions for (x, y, z) are $(1, 1, 0)$; thus, our answer is $100 \times 1 = 100$.

Example 6. (USAMO Modified) Find $100x$ if x and y are real numbers satisfying

the system of equations $\begin{cases} x + y + z = 3 & \text{(1)} \\ x^2 + y^2 + z^2 = 3 & \text{(2)} \\ x^3 + y^3 + z^3 = 3 & \text{(3)} \end{cases}$

Solution: 100.

From (1) and (2): $x + y = 3 - z$ (4)

Squaring both sides of (4):

$$x^2 + 2xy + y^2 = 9 - 6z + z^2 \Rightarrow 2xy = 9 - 6z + z^2 - (x^2 + y^2) \quad \text{(5)}$$

From (2) we get: $x^2 + y^2 = 3 - z^2$ (6)

Substituting (6) into (5) and simplifying: $xy = z^2 - 2z + 3$.

$$S^2 = \frac{1}{2}[(x^2 + y^2) - \frac{1}{2}(x+y)^2] = \frac{1}{2}[\frac{1}{2}(x+y)^2 - 2xy] = -\frac{3}{4}(z-1)^2 \geq 0,$$

$z = 1$, and $x + y = 2$, $xy = 1$. So $x = y = 1$.

Substituting $x = y = z = 1$ into (3): $x = y = z = 1$. The answer is $100 \times 1 = 100$.

2.2. Method of Completing The Squares

Example 7. Find $m^2 + n^2$ if the value of y can be expressed as $\dfrac{m}{n}$, where m and n are positive integers relatively prime and y and z are real numbers satisfying the equation $5y^2 + 5z^2 + 8yz - 6y - 6z + 2 = 0$.

Solution: 010.

The given equation can be written as

$(9y^2 - 6y + 1) + (9z^2 - 6z + 1) = 4y^2 + -8yz + 4z^2$ or

$(3y-1)^2 + (3z-1)^2 = 4(y-z)^2$ \hspace{2cm} (1)

Let $u = 3y - 1$, $v = 3z - 1$.

Then (1) becomes $5u^2 + 8uv + 5v^2 = 0$.

Note that $\Delta = (8v)^2 - 4 \times 5 \times 5v^2 = -36v^2$.

We know that and y and z are real numbers, so we have $v = 0$, and $u = 0$.

$u = 3y - 1 \quad \Rightarrow \quad y = \dfrac{1}{3}$.

$v = 3z - 1 \quad \Rightarrow \quad z = \dfrac{1}{3}$.

$m^2 + n^2 = 1^2 + 3^2 = 10$.

Example 8. Find $100(x + y - z)$ if $x, y,$ and z are real numbers satisfying the system of equations

$x^2 + y^2 + z^2 - 9x - 8y - 5z + 11 = 0$ \hspace{2cm} (1)

$x + 2y + 3z + 1 = 0$ \hspace{2cm} (2)

Solution: 600.

$(1) + (2) \times 3$: $x^2 + y^2 + z^2 - 6x - 2y + 4z + 14 = 0 \quad \Rightarrow$

$(x^2 - 6x + 9) + (y^2 - 2y + 1) + (z^2 + 4z + 4) = 0 \Rightarrow (x-3)^2 + (y-1)^2 + (z+2)^2 = 0$

We know that x, y, and z are real numbers, so we have

$x - 3 = 0 \qquad \Rightarrow \qquad x = 3.$

$y - 1 = 0 \qquad \Rightarrow \qquad y = 1.$

$z + 2 = 0 \qquad \Rightarrow \qquad z = -2.$

$100(x + y - z) = 100 \times 6 = 600.$

2.3. Solving System Of Equations Using Vieta's Theorem

Example 9. Find the number of distinct ordered triples (x, y, z) satisfying the equations

$$x + 2y + 4z = 12$$
$$xy + 4yz + 2xz = 22$$
$$xyz = 6.$$

Solution: 006.

Let $a = x$, $b = 2y$, and $c = 4z$.

$x + 2y + 4z = 12 \qquad\qquad\quad \Rightarrow \qquad a + b + c = 12$

$xy + 4yz + 2xz = 22 \quad \Rightarrow \qquad ab + bc + ca = 44 \qquad\qquad \Big\}$ (4)

$xyz = 6 \qquad\qquad\qquad\quad \Rightarrow \qquad abc = 48$

a, b, and c are the solutions of the equation: $t^3 - 12t^2 + 44t - 48 = 0 \qquad\qquad \Rightarrow$

$(t - 2)(t - 4)(t - 6) = 0$

The triple $(2, 4, 6)$ and each of its permutations satisfies the system (4). Since there is a one-to-one correspondence between (a, b, c) and (x, y, z), the original system has 6 distinct solutions (x, y, z): $(2, 2, \frac{3}{2})$, $(2, 3, 1)$, $(4, 1, \frac{3}{2})$, $(4, 3, \frac{1}{2})$, $(6, 1, 1)$, $(6, 2, \frac{1}{2})$.

3. RATIONAL EQUATIONS

Example 10. Find the largest value of x satisfying $\dfrac{2x^2}{x^2-4} \times (x^2+6) = \dfrac{10x^3}{x^2-4}$.

Solution: 003.

$$\frac{2x^2}{x^2-4} \times (x^2+6) = \frac{10x^3}{x^2-4} \qquad \Rightarrow \qquad \frac{2x^2}{x^2-4} \times (x^2+6) - \frac{10x^3}{x^2-4} = 0 \Rightarrow$$

$$\frac{2x^2}{x^2-4}[(x^2+6)-5x] = 0 \qquad \Rightarrow \qquad \frac{2x^2(x-2)(x-3)}{(x-2)(x+2)} = 0.$$

We know that x – 2 ≠ 0, so we simplify the above equation into: $\dfrac{2x^2(x-3)}{(x+2)} = 0$.

The solutions are $x = 0$ and $x = 3$. We checked and both are the solutions of the equation. The answer is 3.

Example 11. Find the positive value of x satisfying $x^2 + 6 - \dfrac{1}{x-2} = \dfrac{5x^2 - 10x - 1}{x-2}$,

Solution: 003.

The given equation can be written as $x^2 + 6 - \dfrac{1}{x-2} = 5x - \dfrac{1}{x-2} \qquad \Rightarrow$

$x^2 - 5x + 6 = 0 \qquad \Rightarrow (x-2)(x-3) = 0$

Thus $x = 3$ or $x = 2$, but it is obvious that $x \neq 2$. Thus $x = 3$.

☆**Example 12.** Find abc if $\dfrac{3}{a+3} + \dfrac{3}{b+3} + \dfrac{3}{c+3} = 1$ and $a + b + c = 43$.

Solution: 441.

$$\frac{3}{a+3}+\frac{3}{b+3}+\frac{3}{c+3}=1 \qquad \Rightarrow$$

$$\frac{3(b+3)(c+3)+3(a+3)(c+3)+3(a+3)(b+3)}{(a+3)(b+3)(c+3)}=1$$

$$\Rightarrow \qquad 3(b+3)(c+3)+3(a+3)(c+3)+3(a+3)(b+3)=(a+3)(b+3)(c+3)$$

$$\Rightarrow 3(ab+bc+ca)+18(a+b+c)+81=abc+3(ab+bc+ca)+9(a+b+c)+27$$

$$\Rightarrow 9(a+b+c)+54=abc \qquad \Rightarrow abc=9\times 43+54=441.$$

☆**Example 13.** Let m be the largest real solution to the equation

$$\frac{1}{x-1}+\frac{3}{x-3}+\frac{5}{x-5}+\frac{7}{x-7}=x^2-4x-4$$

There are positive integers a, b and c such that $m=a+\sqrt{b+\sqrt{c}}$. Find $a+b+c$.

Solution: 031.

$$\frac{1}{x-1}+\frac{3}{x-3}+\frac{5}{x-5}+\frac{7}{x-7}=x^2-4x-4 \qquad \Rightarrow$$

$$\frac{-(x-1)+x}{x-1}+\frac{-(x-3)+x}{x-3}+\frac{-(x-5)+x}{x-5}+\frac{-(x-7)+x}{x-7}=x^2-4x-4$$

$$\Rightarrow -4+\frac{x}{x-1}+\frac{x}{x-3}+\frac{x}{x-5}+\frac{x}{x-7}=x^2-4x-4\Rightarrow$$

$$\frac{x}{x-1}+\frac{x}{x-3}+\frac{x}{x-5}+\frac{x}{x-7}-x(x-4)\Rightarrow$$

$$x[\frac{1}{x-1}+\frac{1}{x-3}+\frac{1}{x-5}+\frac{1}{x-7}-(x-4)]=0 \qquad\qquad (1)$$

We get $x=0$ or $\dfrac{1}{x-1}+\dfrac{1}{x-3}+\dfrac{1}{x-5}+\dfrac{1}{x-7}-(x-4)=0 \qquad (2)$

Let $y=x-4$ in (2):

$$\frac{1}{y+3}+\frac{1}{y+1}+\frac{1}{y-1}+\frac{1}{y-3}-y=0 \quad \Rightarrow$$

$$(\frac{1}{y+3}+\frac{1}{y-3})+(\frac{1}{y+1}+\frac{1}{y-1})-y=0$$

$$\Rightarrow \quad \frac{2y}{y^2-9}+\frac{2y}{y^2-1}-y=0 \Rightarrow \quad y(\frac{2}{y^2-9}+\frac{2}{y^2-1}-1)=0 \quad (3)$$

We get $y=0$ or $\dfrac{2}{y^2-9}+\dfrac{2}{y^2-1}-1=0$ $\qquad\qquad\qquad$ (4)

Let $z=y^2$, (4) becomes: $\quad \dfrac{2}{z-9}+\dfrac{2}{z-1}-1=0 \quad \Rightarrow \quad \dfrac{2(z-1)+2(z-9)}{(z-9)(z-1)}=1$

$$\Rightarrow \quad 4z-20=(z-9)(z-1) \quad \Rightarrow \quad 4z-20=z^2-10z+9 \quad \Rightarrow$$

$$z^2-14z+29=0$$

Solving we get $z_{1,2}=7\pm2\sqrt{5}$. Since we want the greatest value, we get

$$z=7+2\sqrt{5}$$

Thus $y=\sqrt{7+2\sqrt{5}}$ and $m=4+y=4+\sqrt{7+2\sqrt{5}}=4+\sqrt{7+\sqrt{20}}$

$a+b+c = 4+7+20 = 031$.

Example 14. Let m be the smallest real solution to the equation

$$\frac{1}{x+5}+\frac{2}{x+4}+\frac{3}{x+3}-\frac{3}{x+2}+\frac{2}{x+1}+\frac{1}{x}=0$$

There are positive integers a, b and c such that $m=\dfrac{-a-\sqrt{b}}{c}$ in simplest radical

form. Find $a+b+c$.

Solution: 420.

The original equation can be written as

$$(\frac{1}{x+5}+\frac{1}{x})+(\frac{3}{x+3}-\frac{3}{x+2})+(\frac{2}{x+1}+\frac{2}{x+4})=0 \quad \Rightarrow$$

$$\frac{2x+5}{(x+5)x}-\frac{3(2x+5)}{(x+3)(x+2)}+\frac{2(2x+5)}{(x+1)(x+4)}=0 \Rightarrow$$

$$(2x+5)(\frac{1}{x^2+5x}-\frac{3}{x^2+5x+6}+\frac{2}{x^2+5x+4})=0 \qquad (1)$$

We have $2x+5=0 \quad \Rightarrow \quad x_1=-5/2$.

We have $\dfrac{1}{x^2+5x}+\dfrac{2}{x^2+5x+4}-\dfrac{3}{x^2+5x+6}=0 \qquad (2)$

Let $y=x^2+5x$. (2) becomes $\dfrac{1}{y}+\dfrac{2}{y+4}-\dfrac{3}{y+6}=0 \Rightarrow \dfrac{10y+24}{y(y+4)(y+6)}=0 \Rightarrow$

$y=-\dfrac{12}{5}$.

When $y=-\dfrac{12}{5}$, $x^2+5x=-\dfrac{12}{5} \qquad \Rightarrow \qquad 5x^2+25x+12=0 \qquad (3)$

Solving we get $x_2=\dfrac{-25+\sqrt{385}}{10}$, and $x_3=\dfrac{-25-\sqrt{385}}{10}$.

Since we want the smallest real solution, we get $m=x_3=\dfrac{-25-\sqrt{385}}{10}$

$a+b+c=25+385+10=420$.

☆**Example 15.** (AIME) Find the positive solution

$$\frac{1}{x^2-10x-29}+\frac{1}{x^2-10x-45}-\frac{2}{x^2-10x-69}=0$$

Solution: 013.

Method 1 (official solution):

Let $y=x^2-10x$. The equation in the problem then becomes

$$\frac{1}{y-29}+\frac{1}{y-45}-\frac{2}{y-69}=0$$

From which $\dfrac{1}{y-29} - \dfrac{1}{y-69} = \dfrac{1}{y-69} - \dfrac{1}{y-45} = 0$ and

$\dfrac{-40}{(y-29)(y-69)} = \dfrac{24}{(y-45)(y-69)}$ follows. This equation has $y = 39$ as its only

solution. We then note that $x^2 - 10x = 39$ is satisfied by the positive number 13.

Method 2 (our solution):

The equation in the problem can be written as

$$\frac{1}{x^2 -10x - 29} - \frac{1}{x^2 -10x - 69} = \frac{1}{x^2 -10x - 69} - \frac{1}{x^2 -10x - 45}$$

$\Rightarrow \quad \dfrac{-40}{(x^2 -10x - 29)(x^2 -10x - 69)} = \dfrac{24}{(x^2 -10x - 69)(x^2 -10x - 45)}$

$\Rightarrow \quad -5[(x^2 -10x - 69)(x^2 -10x - 45)] = 3[(x^2 -10x - 29)(x^2 -10x - 69)]$

$\Rightarrow \quad 3[(x^2 -10x - 29)(x^2 -10x - 69)] + 5[(x^2 -10x - 69)(x^2 -10x - 45)] = 0$

$\Rightarrow \quad (x^2 -10x - 69)[3(x^2 -10x - 29) + 5(x^2 -10x - 45)] = 0$

$\Rightarrow \quad (x^2 -10x - 69)(8x^2 - 80x - 312) = 0$

We know that $x^2 -10x - 69 \neq 0$. So $8x^2 - 80x - 312 = 0 \quad \Rightarrow$

$\qquad x^2 -10x - 39 = 0$.

The solutions are $x_1 = 13$ and $x_2 = -3$. The answer is the positive number 13.

Method 3 (our solution):

Let $y = x^2 -10x - 49$. The equation in the problem then becomes

$\dfrac{1}{y+20} + \dfrac{1}{y+4} - \dfrac{2}{y-20} = 0 \quad \Rightarrow$

$\qquad y^2 -16y - 80 + y^2 - 400 - 2y^2 - 48y -160 = 0$

$\Rightarrow \quad -64y = 640 \quad \Rightarrow \quad y = -10$.

So $x^2 -10x - 49 = -10 \qquad \Rightarrow \qquad x^2 -10x - 39 = 0$.

The solutions are $x_1 = 13$ and $x_2 = -3$. The answer is the positive number 13.

Method 4 (our solution):

Let $y = x^2 - 10x - 29$. The equation in the problem then becomes

$$\frac{1}{y} + \frac{1}{y-16} - \frac{2}{y-40} = 0 \qquad \Rightarrow \qquad \frac{1}{y} - \frac{1}{y-40} = \frac{1}{y-40} - \frac{1}{y-16} \Rightarrow$$

$$\frac{-40}{y(y-40)} = \frac{24}{(y-40)(y-16)}$$

$$\frac{-5}{y} = \frac{3}{y-16} \qquad \Rightarrow \qquad y = 10.$$

So $x^2 - 10x - 29 = 10 \Rightarrow \qquad x^2 - 10x - 39 = 0$.

The solutions are $x_1 = 13$ and $x_2 = -3$. The answer is 13.

☆**Example 16.** Find the largest solution to the equation

$$\frac{1}{x^2 + 11x - 8} + \frac{1}{x^2 + 2x - 8} - \frac{1}{x^2 - 13x - 8} = 0.$$

Solution: 008.

Let $y = x^2 - 8$. The equation in the problem then becomes

$$\frac{1}{y + 11x} + \frac{1}{y + 2x} + \frac{1}{y - 13x} = 0 \qquad \Rightarrow \qquad 3y^2 - 147x^2 = 0 \qquad \Rightarrow$$

$$y^2 - 49x^2 = 0$$

So we get $y = \pm 7x$.

When $y = 7x$, $x^2 - 8 = 7x \qquad \Rightarrow \qquad x^2 - 7x - 8 = 0$.

Solving we have $x_1 = 8$ and $x_2 = -1$.

When $y = -7x$, $x^2 - 8 = -7x \Rightarrow \qquad x^2 + 7x - 8 = 0$.

Solving we have $x_3 = -8$ and $x_4 = 1$.

The largest solution is $x_1 = 8$. The answer is 8.

4. RADICAL EQUATIONS

☆**Example 17.** Let m be the largest real solution to the equation

$\dfrac{\sqrt{22x}}{\sqrt{22x-120}} = \dfrac{x}{10-x}$. There are positive integers a, and b such that $m = \dfrac{a}{b}$. Find

$a+b$.

Solution: 063.

Squaring both sides: $\dfrac{22x}{22x-120} = \dfrac{x^2}{(10-x)^2}$ $\Rightarrow$ $\dfrac{11x}{11x-60} - \dfrac{x^2}{(10-x)^2} = 0$

$\Rightarrow$ $x[\dfrac{11}{11x-60} - \dfrac{x}{(10-x)^2}] = 0$

We get $x = 0$ or $\dfrac{11}{11x-60} - \dfrac{x}{(10-x)^2} = 0$ $\Rightarrow$ $11(10-x)^2 - x(11x-60) = 0$

$\Rightarrow$ $11(100 - 20x + x^2) - 11x^2 + 60x = 0$ $\Rightarrow$

$1100 - 220x + 11x^2 - 11x^2 + 60x = 0$

$\Rightarrow$ $1100 - 160x = 0 \Rightarrow$ $x = \dfrac{55}{8}$.

The largest solution is $x = \dfrac{55}{8}$. $a+b = 55 + 8 = 63$.

Example 18. Find the positive real solution to the equation
$x^2 + 4x - 8\sqrt{8x} + 20 = 0$.

Solution: 002.

The original equation can be written as $x^2 - 4x + 4 + 8x - 8\sqrt{8x} + 16 = 0$ $\Rightarrow$

$(x-2)^2 + (\sqrt{8x} - 4)^2 = 0$.

We get $x - 2 = 0$ and $\sqrt{8x} - 4 = 0$. The solution is $x = 2$.

☆**Example 19.** (AIME) What is the product of the real roots of the equation $x^2 + 18x + 30 = 2\sqrt{x^2 + 18x + 45}$.

Solution: 020.

Method 1:

Substitute to simplify. Define u to be the nonnegative number such that $u^2 = x^2 + 18x + 45$. So $u^2 - 15 = 2\sqrt{u^2} = 2u$ (since $u \geq 0$).

$u^2 - 2u - 15 = 0 \qquad \Rightarrow \qquad (u-5)(u+3) = 0$.

Since $u \geq 0$, we have $u = 5$.

$x^2 + 18x + 45 = 5^2 \qquad \Rightarrow \qquad x^2 + 18x + 20 = 0$.

Since $\Delta = 18^2 - 4 \times 20 > 0$, the equation has real solutions and the product is 20.

Method 2 (our solution):

The original equation can be written as

$$x^2 + 18x + 45 - 2\sqrt{x^2 + 18x + 45} - 15 = 0 \Rightarrow$$

$$(\sqrt{x^2 + 18x + 45} + 3)(\sqrt{x^2 + 18x + 45} - 5) = 0$$

So we have $\sqrt{x^2 + 18x + 45} + 3 = 0$ (no real solutions)

$$\sqrt{x^2 + 18x + 45} - 5 = 0 \qquad \Rightarrow \qquad \sqrt{x^2 + 18x + 45} = 5 \qquad \Rightarrow$$

$$x^2 + 18x + 45 = 25$$

$$\Rightarrow \qquad x^2 + 18x + 20 = 0 .$$

Since $\Delta = 18^2 - 4 \times 20 > 0$, the equation has real solutions and the product is 20.

Method 3:

The original equation can be written as

$$x^2 + 18x + 45 - 2\sqrt{x^2 + 18x + 45} + 1 = 16 \Rightarrow (\sqrt{x^2 + 18x + 45} - 1)^2 = 16 .$$

We have $\sqrt{x^2 + 18x + 45} - 1 = -4 \qquad \Rightarrow \qquad \sqrt{x^2 + 18x + 45} = -3$ (no real solutions).

or $\sqrt{x^2 + 18x + 45} - 1 = 4$ $\Rightarrow$ $\sqrt{x^2 + 18x + 45} = 5$ $\Rightarrow$

$\qquad x^2 + 18x + 45 = 25$ $\Rightarrow$ $x^2 + 18x + 20 = 0$.

Since $\Delta = 18^2 - 4 \times 20 > 0$, the equation has real solutions and the product is 20.

PROBLEMS

Problem 1. Find $3x + 2y + 6z$ if x, y, and z satisfy the system of equations

$$\begin{cases} \dfrac{x}{2} = \dfrac{y}{3} = \dfrac{z}{5} & (1) \\ 2x + 3y - z = 16 & (2) \end{cases}$$

☆ **Problem 2.** Find $3u + 2v$ if x, y, z, u, and v satisfy the system of equations

$$2x + y + z + u + v = 8 \tag{1}$$
$$x + 2y + z + u + v = 16 \tag{2}$$
$$x + y + 2z + u + v = 32 \tag{3}$$
$$x + y + z + 2u + v = 64 \tag{4}$$
$$x + y + z + u + 2v = 126 \tag{5}$$

Problem 3. Find $x_1 + 4x_4$ if x_1, x_2, x_3, x_4, x_5 satisfy the system of equations

$$x_1 + 2x_2 + 3x_3 + 4x_4 + 5x_5 = 210 \tag{1}$$
$$x_2 + 2x_3 + 3x_4 + 4x_5 + 5x_1 = 185 \tag{2}$$
$$x_3 + 2x_4 + 3x_5 + 4x_1 + 5x_2 = 110 \tag{3}$$
$$x_4 + 2x_5 + 3x_1 + 4x_2 + 5x_3 = 110 \tag{4}$$
$$x_5 + 2x_1 + 3x_2 + 4x_3 + 5x_4 = 135 \tag{5}$$

Problem 4. Find $8x_1 - 4x_2$ if $x_1, x_2, x_3, x_4, \cdots, x_{100}$ satisfy the system of equations

$$\begin{cases} x_1 + 2x_2 + 2x_3 + 2x_4 + 2x_5 + \cdots + 2x_{100} = 1 & (1) \\ 2x_1 + 2x_2 + 2x_3 + 2x_4 + 2x_5 + \cdots + 2x_{100} = 2 & (2) \\ 2x_1 + 2x_2 + 3x_3 + 2x_4 + 2x_5 + \cdots + 2x_{100} = 3 & (3) \\ 2x_1 + 2x_2 + 2x_3 + 4x_4 + 2x_5 + \cdots + 2x_{100} = 4 & (4) \\ \cdots \quad \cdots \quad \cdots \quad \cdots \quad \cdots \\ 2x_1 + 2x_2 + 2x_3 + 2x_4 + 2x_5 + \cdots + 100x_{100} = 100 & (100) \end{cases}$$

Problem 5: Find $m + n$ if the greatest value of y can be expressed as $\dfrac{m}{n}$, where m and n are positive integers relatively prime and x and y are real numbers satisfying the system of equations

$$\begin{cases} x(x+1)(3x+5y) = 144 \\ x^2 + 4x + 5y = 24. \end{cases}$$

Problem 6. Find $10x + 100z$. x, y, and z are real numbers satisfying the system of equations

$$\begin{cases} 2x + 3y + z = 13 & (1) \\ 4x^2 + 9y^2 + z^2 - 2x + 15y + 3z = 82 & (2) \end{cases}$$

Problem 7. Find $100x^2 + y^2$ if x and y are real numbers satisfying the equation $5x^2 - 6xy + 2y^2 - 4x + 2y + 1 = 0$.

Problem 8. Find $100(x + y + z)$ if x, y, and z are real numbers satisfying the system of equations

$$\begin{cases} 2x + 3y + z = 13 & (1) \\ 4x^2 + 9y^2 + z^2 - 2x + 15y + 3z = 82 & (2) \end{cases}$$

Problem 9. Find $100(x + y)$ if x and y are real numbers satisfying the system of

equations: $\begin{cases} x + y + \dfrac{9}{x} + \dfrac{4}{y} = 10 \\ (x^2 + 9)(y^2 + 4) = 24xy \end{cases}$

Problem 10. Find the positive value of n satisfying $\dfrac{1}{1985} = \dfrac{1}{1 + (1 - \frac{1}{n})^2} \times \dfrac{1}{n^2}$.

Problem 11. Find the positive real value of x satisfying $x^2 - x + 1 = \dfrac{6}{x^2 - x}$.

☆**Problem 12.** Find $1000 + m + n$ if m and n are two nonzero roots of the equation $\dfrac{a}{x+a} + \dfrac{b}{x+b} + \dfrac{c}{x+c} = 3$ with $a + b + c = 12$, and $ab + cb + ac = 47$.

Problem 13. Let m be the largest real solution to the equation
$$\frac{3}{x} + \frac{1}{x-1} + \frac{4}{x-2} + \frac{4}{x-3} + \frac{1}{x-4} + \frac{3}{x-5} = 0$$
There are positive integers a, b and c such that $m = \dfrac{a + \sqrt{b}}{c}$. Find $a+b+c$.

Problem 14. Let m be the real solution to the equation
$29(\dfrac{17-7x}{x+2} + \dfrac{8x+55}{x+3}) = 31(\dfrac{24-5x}{x+1} + \dfrac{5-6x}{x+4}) + 370$. There are positive integers a, and b such that $m = -\dfrac{a}{b}$. Find $a+b$.

Problem 15. Find the largest solution to the equation
$$\frac{1}{x^2 + 2x + 10} + \frac{1}{x^2 + 11x + 10} - \frac{1}{x^2 - 13x + 10} = 0$$

☆**Problem 16.** Find the largest solution to the equation
$$\frac{x-2}{3} + \frac{x-3}{2} = \frac{3}{x-2} + \frac{2}{x-3}.$$

☆**Problem 17.** Find the last three digits of the sum of the solutions of the equation $\sqrt[4]{x} = \dfrac{14}{9 - \sqrt[4]{x}}$.

Problem 18. Find $800m$ if m is the positive solution to the equation

$$x^2 + \frac{1}{x^2} + \sqrt{x^2 + 2 + \frac{1}{x^2}} = 4.$$

☆ **Problem 19.** Let $m = \dfrac{a}{b}$ be the positive real solution to the equation

$2x^2 - 5x - 2x\sqrt{x^2 - 5x - 3} = 19$. a and b are positive integers relatively prime.
Find $a+b$.

Problem 20. How many solutions are there for real x, y, z and u to the system of equations below?

$$\begin{cases} x + y + z + u = 8, & (1) \\ x^2 + y^2 + z^2 + u^2 = 20, & (2) \\ xy + xu + zy + zu = 16, & (3) \\ xyzu = 9. & (4) \end{cases}$$

Problem 21. Given the equation $49(x^2 + 4y^2 + 9z^2) = 36(x + y + z)^2$, x, y, and z are real numbers. $x : y : z$ can be expressed as $a : b : c$, where a, b, and c are positive integers relatively prime. Find $a + b + c$.

SOLUTIONS

Problem 1. Solution: 084.

Let $\dfrac{x}{2} = \dfrac{y}{3} = \dfrac{z}{5} = k$ (3)

$x = 2k$, $y = 3k$, and $z = 5k$. Substituting these values into (2): $4k + 9k - 5k = 16$

$\Rightarrow \quad k = 2$

$3x + 2y + 6z = 6k + 6k + 30k = 42k = 84$

☆ **Problem 2.** Solution: 239.

(1) + (2) + (3) + (4) + (5):

$6(x + y + z + u + v) = 246 \quad \Rightarrow \quad x + y + z + u + v = 41$ (6)

(4) − (6): $u = 23$.

(5) − (6): $v = 85$.

$3u + 2v = 3 \times 23 + 2 \times 85 = 239$.

Problem 3. Solution: 065.

Let $S = x_1 + x_2 + x_3 + x_4 + x_5$.

(1) + (2) + (3) + (4) + (5): $S + 2S + 3S + 4S + 5S = 750 \quad \Rightarrow \quad 15S = 750 \Rightarrow$

$\qquad S = 50$

(1) − (2): $-4x_1 + x_2 + x_3 + x_4 + x_5 = 25 \qquad \Rightarrow x_1 + x_2 + x_3 + x_4 + x_5 - 5x_1 = 25$

$\qquad \Rightarrow x_1 = \dfrac{50 - 25}{5} = 5$

(5) − (4): $-x_1 - x_2 - x_3 + 4x_4 - x_5 = 25 \qquad \Rightarrow -x_1 - x_2 - x_3 - x_4 - x_5 + 5x_4 = 25$

$\qquad \Rightarrow -S + 5x_4 = 25 \qquad \Rightarrow x_4 = \dfrac{50 + 25}{5} = 15$

$x_1 + 4x_4 = 5 + 4 \times 15 = 5 + 60 = 65$.

Problem 4. Solution: 400.

(2) − (1), (3) − (2), (4) − (3), (5) − (4), ... (100) − (99), we get

$$x_1 = 1$$

$$x_3 = 1$$

$$-x_3 + 2x_4 = 1$$

$$-2x_4 + 3x_5 = 1$$

$$\cdots \qquad \cdots \qquad \cdots \qquad \cdots$$

$$-97x_{99} + 98x_{100} = 1$$

So we get the solutions: $x_1 = x_3 = x_4 = \ldots = x_{99} = x_{100} = 1$.

Substituting all these values to equation (2) we get $x_2 = 2 - 100 = -98$.

$8x_1 - 4x_2 = 8 \times 1 - 4 \times (-98) = 400$.

Problem 5. Solution: 029.

Rewrite the equations as: $\begin{cases} (x^2 + x)(3x + 5y) = 144, \\ (x^2 + x) + (3x + 5y) = 24. \end{cases}$

Let $x^2 + x = a$, $3x + 5y = b$. $a + b = 24$, $ab = 144$.

The square of the difference of a and b:

$$s^2 = \frac{1}{2}[(a^2 + b^2) - \frac{1}{2}(a+b)^2] = \frac{1}{2}[\frac{1}{2}(a+b)^2 - 2ab] = \frac{1}{2}(\frac{1}{2} \times 24^2 - 2 \times 144) = 0$$

$a = b = 12$.

So $x^2 + x = 3x + 5y = 12$. Solving: $\begin{cases} x_1 = 3, \\ y_1 = \dfrac{3}{5}; \end{cases} \begin{cases} x_2 = -4, \\ y_2 = \dfrac{24}{5}. \end{cases}$

The greatest value of y is 24/5. The answer is $24 + 5 = 29$.

Problem 6. Solution: 430.

From (1): $2x + (3y + 3) = 16 - z$.   (3)

(1) + (2): $(2x)^2 + (3y + 3)^2 = -z^2 - 4z + 104$ (4)

The square of the difference of $2x$, $3y + 3$

$$S^2 = \frac{1}{2}[(2x)^2 + (3y+3)^2 - \frac{1}{2}(2x + 3y + 3)^2] \geq 0$$ (5)

Substituting (3), (4) into (5): $-3(z-4)^2 \geq 0$ $\Rightarrow$ $z = 4$
Substituting $z = 4$ into (1), (2): $x = 3$, $y = 1$.
The answer is $10x + 100z = 30 + 400 = 430$.

Problem 7. Solution: 101.
The left hand side of the given equation can be written as
$$= (x^2 - 2xy + y^2) + (4x^2 - 4xy + y^2) - 4x + 2y + 1$$
$$= (x-y)^2 + (2x-y)^2 - 2(2x-y) + 1$$
$$= (x-y)^2 + (2x-y-1)^2.$$
So we have $(x-y)^2 + (2x-y-1)^2 = 0$.
We know that x and y are real numbers, so we have
$$(x-y)^2 = 0 \qquad \Rightarrow \qquad x = y$$
$$(2x-y-1)^2 = 0 \qquad \Rightarrow \qquad 2x-y-1 = 0 \Rightarrow \qquad 2x-x-1 = 0 \Rightarrow$$
$$\qquad\qquad x = y = 1.$$
$100x^2 + y^2 = 101$.

Problem 8. Solution: 800.
From (1), we have $2x + 3y = 13 - z$.
Let $2x = \dfrac{13-z}{2} + t$, and $3y = \dfrac{13-z}{2} - t$ (3)

Substituting (3) into (2): $3(z-4)^2 + 4\left(t - \dfrac{3}{2}\right)^2 = 0$.

So $z = 4$ and $t = \dfrac{3}{2}$ (4)

Substituting the values in (4) into (3), we get $x = 3$, $y = 1$. The solution is $x = 3$, $y = 1$, $z = 4$.
$100(x + y + z) = 100 \times 8 = 800$.

Problem 9. Solution: 500.

The given system of equations can be written as

$$\begin{cases} (x+\dfrac{9}{x})+(y+\dfrac{4}{y})=10 & (1) \\[4mm] \left(x+\dfrac{9}{x}\right)\left(y+\dfrac{4}{y}\right)=24 & (2) \end{cases}$$

$x+\dfrac{9}{x}=m$ and $y+\dfrac{4}{y}=n$ are two roots of the quadratic equation: $t^2-10t+24=0.$

So $t_1=4$ and $t_2=6$.

It follows that

$$\begin{cases} x+\dfrac{9}{x}=6 \\[4mm] y+\dfrac{4}{y}=4 \end{cases} \qquad (3)$$

Or

$$\begin{cases} x+\dfrac{9}{x}=4 \\[4mm] y+\dfrac{4}{y}=6 \end{cases} \qquad (4)$$

Solving (3), we get $x=3$, $y=2$. There are no real solutions for (4).
The answer is $100(x+y)=100(2+3)=500$.

Problem 10. Solution: 032.

$$\frac{1}{1985}=\frac{1}{1+(1-\dfrac{1}{n})^2}\times\frac{1}{n^2} \Rightarrow \frac{1}{1985}=\frac{1}{1+(\dfrac{n-1}{n})^2}\times\frac{1}{n^2} \Rightarrow$$

$$\frac{1}{1985}=\frac{1}{1+\dfrac{(n-1)^2}{n^2}}\times\frac{1}{n^2}$$

$$\Rightarrow \quad \frac{1}{1985} = \frac{1}{\dfrac{n^2+(n-1)^2}{n^2}} \times \frac{1}{n^2} \qquad \Rightarrow \quad \frac{1}{1985} = \frac{1}{n^2+(n-1)^2}$$

$$\Rightarrow \quad n^2+(n-1)^2 = 1985 \qquad \Rightarrow \quad n^2+n^2-2n+1 = 1985$$

$$\Rightarrow \quad 2n^2-2n-1984 = 0 \qquad \Rightarrow \quad n^2-n-992 = 0 \qquad \Rightarrow (n-32)(n+31) = 0$$

The positive value of n is 32.

Problem 11. Solution: 002.

Let $y = x^2 - x$. The given equation becomes: $y+1 = \dfrac{6}{y} \Rightarrow y^2+y-6 = 0$

$$\Rightarrow (y-2)(y+3) = 0$$

So $y = 2$ or $y = -3$.

So we have $x^2 - x = -3 \qquad \Rightarrow \qquad x^2-x+3 = 0$ (no real solution).

$x^2 - x = 2 \qquad \Rightarrow \qquad x^2-x-2 = 0$.

So $x = 2$ or $x = -1$.

We have checked and both are the solutions. The answer is $x = 2$.

☆**Problem 12.** Solution: 992.

$$\frac{a}{x+a}+\frac{b}{x+b}+\frac{c}{x+c} = 3 \qquad \Rightarrow \qquad (1-\frac{a}{x+a})+(1-\frac{b}{x+b})+(1-\frac{c}{x+c}) = 0$$

$$\Rightarrow \qquad \frac{x}{x+a}+\frac{x}{x+b}+\frac{x}{x+c} = 0 \qquad \Rightarrow$$

$$\frac{x[3x^2+2(a+b+c)x+(ab+bc+ca)]}{(x+a)(x+b)(x+c)} = 0.$$

We have $x = 0$ or

$$3x^2+2(a+b+c)x+(ab+bc+ca) = 0 \qquad \Rightarrow \qquad 3x^2+24x+47 = 0.$$

The sum of the roots is $m+n = -\dfrac{24}{3} = -8$

The answer is $1000 + m + n = 1000 - 8 = 992$.

Problem 13. Solution: 024.

The original equation can be written as

$$3(\frac{1}{x}+\frac{1}{x-5})+(\frac{1}{x-1}+\frac{1}{x-4})+4(\frac{1}{x-2}+\frac{1}{x-3})=0 \quad \Rightarrow$$

$$\frac{3(2x-5)}{x(x-5)}+\frac{2x-5}{(x-1)(x-4)}+\frac{4(2x-5)}{(x-2)(x-3)}=0$$

$$\Rightarrow \quad (2x-5)[\frac{3}{x(x-5)}+\frac{1}{(x-1)(x-4)}+\frac{4}{(x-2)(x-3)}]=0 \qquad (1)$$

We have $2x-5=0 \quad \Rightarrow \quad x_1=5/2.$

We have $\dfrac{3}{x(x-5)}+\dfrac{1}{(x-1)(x-4)}+\dfrac{4}{(x-2)(x-3)}=0 \qquad \Rightarrow$

$$\frac{3}{x^2-5x}+\frac{1}{x^2-5x+4}+\frac{4}{x^2-5x+6}=0 \qquad (2)$$

Let $y=x^2-5x$. (2) becomes $\dfrac{3}{y}+\dfrac{1}{y+4}+\dfrac{4}{y+6}=0 \Rightarrow \quad 2y^2+13y+18=0$

$$\Rightarrow \quad (y+2)(2y+9)=0$$

We get $y=-2$ or $y=-\dfrac{9}{2}$.

When $y=-2$, $x^2-5x=-2 \quad \Rightarrow \qquad x^2-5x+2=0$

Solving we get $x_2=\dfrac{5+\sqrt{17}}{2}$, and $x_3=\dfrac{5-\sqrt{17}}{2}$.

When $y=-\dfrac{9}{2}$, $x^2-5x=-\dfrac{9}{2} \Rightarrow \qquad 2x^2-10x+9=0$

Solving we get $x_4=\dfrac{5+\sqrt{7}}{2}$, and $x_5=\dfrac{5-\sqrt{7}}{2}$.

Since we want the greatest real solution, we get $m=x_2=\dfrac{5+\sqrt{17}}{2}$

$a+b+c=5+17+2=24.$

Problem 14. Solution: 007.

The original equation can be written as

$$29(\frac{31}{x+2} - 7 + \frac{31}{x+3} + 8) = 31(\frac{29}{x+1} - 5 + \frac{29}{x+4} - 6) + 370 \quad \Rightarrow$$

$$29 \times 31(\frac{1}{x+2} + \frac{1}{x+3}) = 31 \times 29(\frac{1}{x+1} + \frac{1}{x+4}) \quad \Rightarrow$$

$$\frac{1}{x+2} + \frac{1}{x+3} = \frac{1}{x+1} + \frac{1}{x+4}$$

$$\Rightarrow \quad \frac{1}{x+1} - \frac{1}{x+3} = \frac{1}{x+2} - \frac{1}{x+4} \quad \Rightarrow \quad \frac{2}{(x+1)(x+3)} = \frac{2}{(x+2)(x+4)} \quad \Rightarrow$$

$$(x+1)(x+3) = (x+2)(x+4) \quad \Rightarrow \quad x^2 + 4x + 3 = x^2 + 6x + 8 \quad \Rightarrow$$

$$x = -\frac{5}{2}. \text{ The answer is } 5 + 2 = 7.$$

Problem 15. Solution: 005.

Let $y = x^2 + 10$. The equation in the problem then becomes

$$\frac{1}{y+2x} + \frac{1}{y+11x} + \frac{1}{y-13x} = 0 \quad \Rightarrow \quad y^2 - 49x^2 = 0$$

So we get $y = \pm 7x$.

When $y = 7x$, $x^2 + 10 = 7x \quad \Rightarrow \quad x^2 - 7x + 10 = 0$.

Solving we have $x_1 = 2$ and $x_2 = 5$.

When $y = -7x$, $x^2 + 10 = -7x \quad \Rightarrow \quad x^2 + 7x + 10 = 0$.

Solving we have $x_3 = -2$ and $x_4 = -5$.

The largest solution is $x_2 = 5$. The answer is 5.

☆**Problem 16.** Solution: 005.

Let $u = \frac{x-2}{3}$, $v = \frac{x-3}{2}$. The equation in the problem then becomes $u + v = \frac{1}{u} + \frac{1}{v}$

$$\Rightarrow \quad (uv - 1)(u + v) = 0.$$

So we have $u + v = 0 \Rightarrow$ $\dfrac{x-2}{3} + \dfrac{x-3}{2} = 0$ $\Rightarrow$ $x = \dfrac{13}{5}$

and $uv = 1$ $\Rightarrow$ $\dfrac{x-2}{3} \times \dfrac{x-3}{2} = 1$ $\Rightarrow$ $x = 5$.

The answer is 5.

☆**Problem 17.** Solution: 417.

$\sqrt[4]{x} = \dfrac{14}{9 - \sqrt[4]{x}}$ $\Rightarrow$ $\sqrt[4]{x}(9 - \sqrt[4]{x}) = 14$ (1)

Let $y = \sqrt[4]{x}$. (1) becomes $y(9 - y) = 14 \Rightarrow$ $y^2 - 9y + 14 = 0$.
Solving we get $y = 7$ or $y = 2$. And $x = 7^4$ or $x = 2^4$.

The sum of the solutions is $7^4 + 2^4 = 2401 + 16 = 2417$. The answer is 417.

Problem 18. Solution: 800.

Let $y = \sqrt{x^2 + 2 + \dfrac{1}{x^2}}$. So $y^2 = x^2 + 2 + \dfrac{1}{x^2}$ $\Rightarrow$ $y^2 - 2 = x^2 + \dfrac{1}{x^2}$.

The original equation becomes $y^2 - 2 + y = 4$ $\Rightarrow$ $y^2 + y - 6 = 0$.
Solving we get $y_1 = -3, y_2 = 2$.

When $y_1 = -3$, $\sqrt{x^2 + 2 + \dfrac{1}{x^2}} = -3$ (no real solutions).

When $y_2 = 2$, $\sqrt{x^2 + 2 + \dfrac{1}{x^2}} = 2 \Rightarrow x^2 + 2 + \dfrac{1}{x^2} = 4 \Rightarrow (x + \dfrac{1}{x})^2 = 4$

        (1)

Since we like to find the positive solution, from (1), we have $x + \dfrac{1}{x} = 2$ $\Rightarrow$

        $x^2 - 2x + 1 = 0$ $\Rightarrow$ $x = 1$.
The answer is $800 \times 1 = 800$.

☆ **Problem 19.** Solution: 032.

Let $y = \sqrt{x^2 - 5x - 3}$. The equation in the problem can be written as

$$y^2 - 2xy + x^2 = 16 \quad \Rightarrow \quad (x - y)^2 = 16 \quad \Rightarrow \quad x - y = -4 \text{ or } \Rightarrow$$
$$x - y = 4.$$

For $x - y = -4$, $x - \sqrt{x^2 - 5x - 3} = -4 \Rightarrow x + 4 = \sqrt{x^2 - 5x - 3} \Rightarrow$

$$(x + 4)^2 = x^2 - 5x - 3 \quad \Rightarrow \quad x^2 + 8x + 16 = x^2 - 5x - 3 \quad \Rightarrow$$

$$13x = -19 \quad \Rightarrow \quad x = -\frac{19}{13}$$

For $x - y = 4$, $x - \sqrt{x^2 - 5x - 3} = 4 \Rightarrow x - 4 = \sqrt{x^2 - 5x - 3} \Rightarrow$

$$(x - 4)^2 = x^2 - 5x - 3 \quad \Rightarrow \quad x^2 - 8x + 16 = x^2 - 5x - 3 \quad \Rightarrow$$

$$-3x = -19 \quad \Rightarrow \quad x = \frac{19}{13}.$$

$a + b = 19 + 13 = 32.$

Problem 20. Solution: 004.

Factoring (3), we have $(x + z) \cdot (y + u) = 16$.   (5)

From (1), (5) we have $\begin{cases} (x + z) + (y + u) = 8 \\ (x + z) \cdot (y + u) = 16. \end{cases}$

Taking $x + z$, $y + u$ as unknowns, based on the Vieta formula, we have

$$\begin{cases} x + z = 4, & (6) \\ y + u = 4. & (7) \end{cases}$$

We complete the square for (2): $(x + z)^2 - 2xz + (y + u)^2 - 2yu = 20$.
Or $16 - 2xz + 16 - 2yu = 20$.
So $xz + yu = 6$ (8)

From (8), (4), we have $\begin{cases} xz + yu = 6 \\ (xz) \cdot (yu) = 9 \end{cases}$.

Taking xz, yu as unknowns, based on the Vieta formula, we have

$$\begin{cases} xz = 3, & (9) \\ yu = 3. & (10) \end{cases}$$

We know from (6), (9) and (7), (10) that x, z or y, u are two roots of $t^2 - 4t + 3 = 0$, so the solutions are $(x, y, z, u) = (1, 1, 3, 3), (3, 1, 1, 3), (1, 3, 3, 1), (3, 3, 1, 1)$.

Problem 21. Solution: 049.

Expanding the equation and cancelling the like terms, we get

$13x^2 + 160y^2 + 405z^2 - 72((xy + yz + zx) = 0$.

Completing the squares: $(3x - 12y)^2 + (4y - 9z)^2 + (18z - 2x)^2 = 0$.

Since x, y, and z are real numbers, we have

$3x - 12y = 0 \quad \Rightarrow \quad x : y = 4 : 1$

$4y - 9z = 0 \quad \Rightarrow \quad y : z = 9 : 4$

So $x : y : z = 36 : 9 : 4$.

The answer is $36 + 9 + 4 = 49$.

BASIC KNOWLEDGE

1.1. Cauchy's Inequality

Let $a_1, a_2, a_3, ..., a_n$ and $b_1, b_2, b_3, ..., b_n$ be real numbers. Then

$$(a_1^2 + a_2^2 + ... + a_n^2) \cdot (b_1^2 + b_2^2 + ... + b_n^2) \ge (a_1 b_1 + a_2 b_2 + ... + a_n b_n)^2$$

(1.1.1)

Equality occurs if and only if $b_i = 0$ ($i = 1, 2, ..., n$) or $a_i = k b_i$ ($i = 1, 2, ..., n$).

Note:

(1). $a_i = k b_i$ ($i = 1, 2, ..., n$) is equivalent to: $\dfrac{a_1}{b_1} = \dfrac{a_2}{b_2} = \cdots = \dfrac{a_n}{b_n}$.

(2). An easy way to memorize the Cauchy's inequality is in the form

$$\sum a^2 \sum b^2 \ge \left(\sum ab \right)^2,$$ which actually means $\displaystyle\sum_{i=1}^{n} a_i^2 \sum_{i=1}^{n} b_i^2 \ge \left(\sum_{i=1}^{n} a_i b_i \right)^2.$

1.2. Proof of Cauchy's Inequality

When $a_1 = a_2 = a_3 = ... = a_n = 0$ or $b_1 = b_2 = b_3 = ... = b_n = 0$, the inequality is true.

Let at least one of $a_1, a_2, a_3, ..., a_n$ not be zero. Then $a_1^2 + a_2^2 + a_3^2 + ... + a_n^2 > 0$.
Consider a quadratic function

$$f(x) = (a_1^2 + a_2^2 + a_3^2 + ... + a_n^2)x^2 + 2(a_1 b_1 + a_2 b_2 + ... + a_n b_n)x +$$
$$(b_1^2 + b_2^2 + b_3^2 + ... + b_n^2).$$

For any real x, $f(x) = (a_1 x + b_1)^2 + (a_2 x + b_2)^2 + ... + (a_n x + b_n)^2 \ge 0$.

Therefore the discriminant of the quadratic function $f(x)$ is less than or equal to zero. That is,

$$4(a_1 b_1 + a_2 b_2 + ... + a_n b_n)^2 - 4(a_1^2 + a_2^2 + ... + a_n^2).(b_1^2 + b_2^2 + ... + b_n^2) \le 0$$
$$\Rightarrow (a_1^2 + a_2^2 + ... + a_n^2) \cdot (b_1^2 + b_2^2 + ... + b_n^2) \ge (a_1 b_1 + a_2 b_2 + ... + a_n b_n)^2.$$

Equality occurs if and only if when $f(x) = 0$ has one real root, which is when $\Delta = 0$.

When this happens, there is only one real x such that $a_i x + b_i = 0$, $(i = 1, 2, ..., n)$. If $x = 0$, then $b_1 = b_2 = b_3 = ... = b_n = 0$, and Cauchy's inequality is true. If $x \neq 0$, then we have $a_i = -\dfrac{1}{x} b_i$. Thus equality occurs if and only if $b_i = 0$ $(i = 1, 2, ..., n)$ or $a_i = k b_i$ $(i = 1, 2, ..., n)$.

1.3. Other Forms of Cauchy's Inequality

1.3.1. If a, b, c, d are real numbers, then $(a^2 + b^2)(c^2 + d^2) \geq (ac + bd)^2$. Equality occurs if and only if $ad = bc$.

Proof:
Method 1:
$$(a^2 + c^2)(b^2 + d^2) - (ab + cd)^2 = (ad - bc)^2 \geq 0.$$
Thus equality occurs if and only if $a = bk$, $c = dk$, where k is real.

Method 2:
If $a^2 + c^2 = 0$, then above inequality is true.
Now consider the case when $a^2 + c^2 \neq 0$.
We consider the quadratic function
$$(ax - b)^2 + (cx - d)^2 = (a^2 + c^2)x^2 - 2(ab + cd)x + (b^2 + d^2) \geq 0,$$
which is positive for all real x.
Therefore the discriminant $\Delta = 4(ab + cd)^2 - 4(a^2 + c^2)(b^2 + d^2) \leq 0$.
Thus $(a^2 + b^2)(c^2 + d^2) \geq (ac + bd)^2$.

1.3.2. If a, b, x, y are real numbers and x, y are positive, then $\dfrac{a^2}{x} + \dfrac{b^2}{y} \geq \dfrac{(a+b)^2}{x+y}$.

Equality occurs if and only if $\dfrac{a}{x} = \dfrac{b}{y}$.

Proof:

Since x, y are positive, the inequality can be written as

$a^2 y (x + y) + b^2 x (x + y) \geq (a + b)^2 xy.$

$a^2 xy + a^2 y^2 + b^2 x^2 + b^2 xy \geq a^2 xy + 2abxy + b^2 xy \qquad \Rightarrow \quad a^2 y^2 + b^2 x^2 \geq 2abxy$

$\Rightarrow$

$(ay - bx)^2 \geq 0$ which is true.

Equality occurs if and only if $ay - bx = 0$ or $\dfrac{a}{x} = \dfrac{b}{y}$.

1.3.3. If a, b, x, y are real numbers and x, y are positive, then

$\dfrac{a^2}{x} + \dfrac{b^2}{y} + \dfrac{c^2}{z} \geq \dfrac{(a+b+c)^2}{x+y+z}$. Equality occurs if and only if $\dfrac{a}{x} = \dfrac{b}{y} = \dfrac{c}{z}$.

1.3.4. Let $a_i \in R$, $b_i > 0$ $(i = 1, 2, ..., n)$. Then

$\dfrac{a_1^2}{b_1} + \dfrac{a_2^2}{b_2} + ... + \dfrac{a_n^2}{b_n} \geq \dfrac{(a_1 + a_2 + ... + a_n)^2}{b_1 + b_2 + ... + b_n}$. Equality occurs if and only if

$\dfrac{a_1}{b_1} = \dfrac{a_2}{b_2} = \cdots = \dfrac{a_n}{b_n}$.

1.3.5. Let a_i and b_i $(i = 1, 2)$ be nonzero real numbers that have the same sign,

then $\dfrac{a_1}{b_1} + \dfrac{a_2}{b_2} \geq \dfrac{(a_1 + a_2)^2}{a_1 b_1 + a_2 b_2}$. Equality occurs if and only if $b_1 = b_2$.

Proof:
Method 1:

114

Since a_1, a_2, b_1, and b_2 have the same sign, we have:

$$\left(a_1 b_1 + a_2 b_2\right)\left(\frac{a_1}{b_1} + \frac{a_2}{b_2}\right) \geq (a_1 + a_2)^2 \text{, or}$$

$$a_1^2 + \frac{a_1 a_2 b_2}{b_1} + \frac{a_1 a_2 b_1}{b_2} + a_2^2 \geq a_1^2 + 2a_1 a_2 + a_2^2 \quad \Rightarrow \quad \frac{a_1 a_2 b_2}{b_1} + \frac{a_1 a_2 b_1}{b_2} \geq 2a_1 a_2$$

$$\Rightarrow \quad \frac{a_1 a_2 b_2}{b_1} + \frac{a_1 a_2 b_1}{b_2} - 2a_1 a_2 \geq 0 \quad \Rightarrow \quad \left(\frac{b_1^2 - 2b_1 b_2 + b_2^2}{b_1 b_2}\right) a_1 a_2 \geq 0 \quad \Rightarrow$$

$$\frac{(b_1 - b_2)^2}{b_1 b_2} a_1 a_2 \geq 0 \, .$$

This is true since $a_1 a_2$ and $b_1 b_2$ are positive.

Equality occurs if and only if $b_1 - b_2 = 0$ or $b_1 = b_2$.

Method 2:

Since none of a_1 and a_2 is zero, we have $\dfrac{a_1}{b_1} + \dfrac{a_2}{b_2} = \dfrac{a_1^2}{a_1 b_1} + \dfrac{a_2^2}{a_2 b_2}$.

By **1.3.2,** we have: $\dfrac{a_1}{b_1} + \dfrac{a_2}{b_2} = \dfrac{a_1^2}{a_1 b_1} + \dfrac{a_2^2}{a_2 b_2} \geq \dfrac{(a_1 + a_2)^2}{a_1 b_1 + a_2 b_2}$.

Equality occurs if and only if $\dfrac{a_1}{a_1 b_1} = \dfrac{a_2}{a_2 b_2}$ or $b_1 = b_2$.

1.3.6. If a_i and b_i $(i = 1, 2, 3)$ are nonzero and have the same sign, then

$\dfrac{a_1}{b_1} + \dfrac{a_2}{b_2} + \dfrac{a_3}{b_3} \geq \dfrac{(a_1 + a_2 + a_3)^2}{a_1 b_1 + a_2 b_2 + a_3 b_3}$. Equality occurs if and only if $b_1 = b_2 = b_3$.

1.3.7. If a_i and b_i $(i = 1, 2, ..., n)$ are nonzero and have the same sign, then

$\dfrac{a_1}{b_1} + \dfrac{a_2}{b_2} + ... + \dfrac{a_n}{b_n} \geq \dfrac{(a_1 + a_2 + ... + a_n)^2}{a_1 b_1 + a_2 b_2 + ... + a_n b_n}$. Equality occurs if and only if

$b_1 = b_2 = ... = b_n$.

APPLICATION OF CAUCHY'S INEQUALITY

2.1. Find The Maximum and Minimum Values

Example 1. If $x + 2y + 3z = 4$, then the smallest value of $x^2 + y^2 + z^2$ is a/b, where a and b are positive integers that are relatively prime. Find $a + b$.

Solution: 015.
By Cauchy's 1.3.3,
$$x^2 + y^2 + z^2 = \frac{x^2}{1} + \frac{(2y)^2}{4} + \frac{(3z)^2}{9} \geq \frac{(x+2y+3z)^2}{1+4+9} = \frac{4^2}{14} = \frac{8}{7}.$$
Equality occurs when $x = \frac{2}{7}, y = \frac{4}{7}, z = \frac{6}{7}$. The smallest value is 8/7. The answer is $8 + 7 = 15$.

Example 2. The smallest value of $x + y$ for $x, y \in R^+$ can be expressed as $a + b\sqrt{c}$ in simplest radical form. Given that $\frac{19}{x} + \frac{98}{y} = 1$, find $a + b + c$.

Solution: 169.
$$1 = \frac{19}{x} + \frac{98}{y} = \frac{(\sqrt{19})^2}{x} + \frac{(\sqrt{98})^2}{y}.$$

By Cauchy's (1.3.2), we have $1 \geq \dfrac{(\sqrt{19} + \sqrt{98})^2}{x+y} = \dfrac{19 + 98 + 14\sqrt{38}}{x+y}$,

Thus $x + y \geq 117 + 14\sqrt{38}$.

Equality occurs when $\dfrac{\sqrt{19}}{x}=\dfrac{\sqrt{98}}{y}$. That is , when $x=19+7\sqrt{38}$, and

$y=98+7\sqrt{38}$, $x+y$ has the smallest value of $117+14\sqrt{38}$. The answer is $117 + 14 + 38 = 169$.

Example 3. Find the smallest value of $x+\dfrac{y}{2}+\dfrac{z}{3}$ if $\dfrac{1}{x}+\dfrac{2}{y}+\dfrac{3}{z}=1$, and $x, y, z \in$

R^{+}.

Solution: 009.

$$\frac{1}{x}+\frac{2}{y}+\frac{3}{z}=1 \Rightarrow \frac{1^2}{x}+\frac{1^2}{\dfrac{y}{2}}+\frac{1^2}{\dfrac{z}{3}}=1 \Rightarrow 1\geq \frac{(1+1+1)^2}{x+\dfrac{y}{2}+\dfrac{z}{3}} \Rightarrow x+\frac{y}{2}+\frac{z}{3}\geq 9.$$

Equality occurs when $\dfrac{1}{x}=\dfrac{1}{\dfrac{y}{2}}=\dfrac{1}{\dfrac{z}{3}}$ or $x = 3, y = 6, z = 9$.

So $(x+\dfrac{y}{2}+\dfrac{z}{3})_{\min} =9$.

Example 4. The largest value of $2x - 3y$ can be written as $a+b\sqrt{c}$ in simplest radical form. Find $a + b + c$ if $x^2 + y^2 = 6x - 4y - 9$.

Solution: 027.
Let $2x - 3y = k$.
$$x^2 + y^2 = 6x - 4y - 9 \Rightarrow (x-3)^2 + (y+2)^2 = 4 \Rightarrow$$
$$\frac{(2x-6)^2}{4}+\frac{(-3y-6)^2}{9}=4$$

By Cauchy's (1.3.3), $4=\dfrac{(2x-6)^2}{4}+\dfrac{(-3y-6)^2}{9}\geq \dfrac{(2x-6-3y-6)^2}{4+9}=\dfrac{(k-12)^2}{13}$,

or

$\dfrac{(k-12)^2}{13} \le 4 \;\Rightarrow\; (k-12)^2 \le 4 \times 13.$

Since we want to find the largest value of k, we get $k \le 12 + 2\sqrt{13}$. The largest

value is then $k = 12 + 2\sqrt{13}$, which is obtained when $x = 3 + \dfrac{4\sqrt{13}}{13}$ and

$y = -2 - \dfrac{6\sqrt{13}}{13}$. These values of x and y can be found by solving the system of

equations $2x - 3y = 12 + 2\sqrt{13}$ and $\dfrac{2x-6}{4} = \dfrac{-3y-6}{9}$. The answer is $12 + 2 + 13$

$= 27.$

Example 5. Find the smallest value of $(x-3)^2 + (y+2)^2$ if $x + 2y - 4 = 0$.

Solution: 5.

$(x-3)^2 + (y+2)^2 = \dfrac{(x-3)^2}{1} + \dfrac{(2y+4)^2}{4}.$

By Cauchy's (1.3.3), we have

$\dfrac{(x-3)^2}{1} + \dfrac{(2y+4)^2}{4} \ge \dfrac{(x-3+2y+4)^2}{1+4} = \dfrac{(4-3+4)^2}{5} = \dfrac{(5)^2}{5} = 5.$

By solving the system of equations:

$$\begin{cases} x + 2y - 4 = 0 \\[2mm] \dfrac{x-3}{1} = \dfrac{2y+4}{4} \end{cases}$$

We get tht $x = 4$ and $y = 0$. Therefore, the smallest value is 5, which is obtained
when $x = 4$ and $y = 0$.

Example 6. The greatest value of $y = 5\sqrt{x-1} + \sqrt{10-2x}$ is $a\sqrt{b}$ in simplest

radical form, where both a and b are positive real numbers. Find $a + b$.

Solution: 009.

The domain of the function is $[1, 5]$, and $y > 0$.

$y = 5\sqrt{x-1} + \sqrt{2}\sqrt{5-x} \le \sqrt{5^2 + (\sqrt{2})^2} \cdot \sqrt{(\sqrt{x-1})^2 + (\sqrt{5-x})^2}$, or $y \le 6\sqrt{3}$.

Equality occurs when $\sqrt{2} \cdot \sqrt{x-1} = 5 \cdot \sqrt{5-x}$ or $x = \dfrac{127}{27}$.

The greatest value of y is $6\sqrt{3}$. Thus the answer is $6 + 3 = 009$.

Example 7. The greatest value of $\sqrt{\dfrac{a}{x}} + 2\sqrt{\dfrac{b}{y}} + 3\sqrt{\dfrac{c}{z}}$ is $s\sqrt{t}$ in simplest rdical

form if $a + 2b + 3c = 4$ and $\dfrac{1}{x} + \dfrac{2}{y} + \dfrac{3}{z} = 8$. $a, b, c, x, y, z \in R^+$. Find $s + t$.

Solution: 006

$a + 2b + 3c = 4 \Rightarrow (\sqrt{a})^2 + (\sqrt{2b})^2 + (\sqrt{3c})^2 = 4$

$\dfrac{1}{x} + \dfrac{2}{y} + \dfrac{3}{z} = 8 \Rightarrow \left(\sqrt{\dfrac{1}{x}}\right)^2 + \left(\sqrt{\dfrac{2}{y}}\right)^2 + \left(\sqrt{\dfrac{3}{z}}\right)^2 = 8.$

From Cauchy's:

$\sqrt{\dfrac{a}{x}} + 2\sqrt{\dfrac{b}{y}} + 3\sqrt{\dfrac{c}{z}} = \sqrt{a} \cdot \sqrt{\dfrac{1}{x}} + \sqrt{2b} \cdot \sqrt{\dfrac{2}{y}} + \sqrt{3c} \cdot \sqrt{\dfrac{3}{z}} \le \sqrt{4 \times 8} = 4\sqrt{2},$

Equality occurs when $\sqrt{\dfrac{8}{4}}\sqrt{a} = \sqrt{\dfrac{1}{x}}$, $\sqrt{\dfrac{8}{4}}\sqrt{2b} = \sqrt{\dfrac{2}{y}}$, $\sqrt{\dfrac{8}{4}}\sqrt{3c} = \sqrt{\dfrac{3}{z}}$,

or $ax = by = cz = \dfrac{1}{2}$. Thus $\left(\sqrt{\dfrac{a}{x}} + 2\sqrt{\dfrac{b}{y}} + 3\sqrt{\dfrac{c}{z}}\right)_{\max} = 4\sqrt{2}.$

The answer is $s + t = 4 + 2 = 6$.

Example 8. (USAMO) The sum of 5 real numbers is 8 and the sum of their squares is 16. What is the largest possible value for one of the numbers?

Solution: $\dfrac{16}{5}$.

Let the five numbers be a, b, c, d, e.

We have $a + b + c + d + e = 8$, and $a^2 + b^2 + c^2 + d^2 + e^2 = 16$.

By Cauchy's Inequality,

$$a^2 + b^2 + c^2 + d^2 = \frac{a^2}{1} + \frac{b^2}{1} + \frac{c^2}{1} + \frac{d^2}{1} \ge \frac{(a+b+c+d)^2}{1+1+1+1} \text{ , or}$$

$$(a+b+c+d)^2 \le 4(a^2 + b^2 + c^2 + d^2).$$

Since $a + b + c + d = 8 - e$ and $a^2 + b^2 + c^2 + d^2 = 16 - e^2$, we have

$$(8-e)^2 \le 4(16 - e^2) \Rightarrow 5e^2 - 16e \le 0 \Rightarrow 0 \le e \le \frac{16}{5}. \text{ When } a = b = c = d = \frac{6}{5},$$

$e_{max} = \dfrac{16}{5}$.

2.2. Solving Analytic Geometry Problems

Example 9. (2004 China Hope Cup Math Contest) **The** greatest value of $x + y$ can be written in the form $\sqrt{a} - b$, where a and b are positive real numbers and a is not a perfect square, given that the point $P(x, y)$ is on the ellipse $\dfrac{(x+2)^2}{4} + (y+1)^2 = 1$. Find $a + b$.

Solution: 008.

Method 1 (official solution):

Let $x = -2 + 2\cos\theta$, and $y = -1 + \sin\theta$, where $0 \le \theta < 2\pi$.

Then, $x + y = -3 + 2\cos\theta + \sin\theta = -3 + \sqrt{5}\sin(\theta + \varphi)$, where $\varphi = \arctan 2$.

The greatest value occurs when $\sin(\theta + \varphi) = 1$. Thus the answer is $5 + 3 = 8$.

Method 2 (our solution):

By Cauchy, we have $\dfrac{(x+2)^2}{4}+\dfrac{(y+1)^2}{1}\geq\dfrac{(x+2+y+1)^2}{4+1}=\dfrac{(x+y+3)^2}{5}$.

Thus $\dfrac{(x+y+3)^2}{5}\leq1\ \Rightarrow\qquad(x+y+3)^2\leq5\qquad\Rightarrow\qquad x+y+3\leq\sqrt{5}\Rightarrow$

$x+y\leq\sqrt{5}-3$.

Equality occurs if and only if $\dfrac{x+2}{4}=\dfrac{y+1}{1}\quad\Rightarrow\qquad\dfrac{x+2}{4}=y+1$

Substituting $\dfrac{x+2}{4}=y+1$ into the equation of the ellipse, we obtain that:

$x=\dfrac{4\sqrt{5}}{5}-2$ and $y=\dfrac{\sqrt{5}}{5}-1$. The answer is $5+3=008$.

Example 10. P is a point on the ellipse $\dfrac{x^2}{4}+\dfrac{y^2}{7}=1$ so that the distance from P to

the line l: $3x-2y-16=0$ is the shortest. Find $a+b+c+d$ if the coordnates of

P are $(\dfrac{a}{b},-\dfrac{c}{d})$.

Solution: 16.
The distance from a point on the ellipse to the line is

$d=\dfrac{|3x-2y-16|}{\sqrt{3^2+(-2)^2}}=\dfrac{|3x-2y-16|}{\sqrt{13}}$.

Since we want to find the smallest value of d, we want to find the greatest value
of $3x-2y$ so that the numerator is as small as possible.

We rewrite $\dfrac{x^2}{4}+\dfrac{y^2}{7}=1$ as $\dfrac{(3x)^2}{4\times3^2}+\dfrac{(-2y)^2}{7\times2^2}=1$.

By Cauchy's Inequality, $\dfrac{(3x)^2}{4\times3^2}+\dfrac{(-2y)^2}{7\times2^2}\geq\dfrac{(3x-2y)^2}{36+28}=\dfrac{(3x-2y)^2}{64}$.

Thus $1\geq\dfrac{(3x-2y)^2}{64}$.

It follows that $(3x - 2y)^2 \leq 64$ $\Rightarrow$ $3x - 2y \leq 8$.

The greatest value of $3x - 2y$ is 8.

Equality occurs when $\dfrac{3x}{36} = \dfrac{-2y}{28}$, or $x = \dfrac{3}{2}$ and $y = -\dfrac{7}{4}$. The answer is $3 + 2 + 7$

$+ 4 = 016$. (The shortest distance is $d = \dfrac{8}{\sqrt{13}} = \dfrac{8\sqrt{13}}{13}$).

Example 11. Point (x, y) is on the ellipse $4(x - 2)^2 + y^2 = 4$. The smallest value of

y/x can be written as $-\dfrac{a\sqrt{b}}{c}$ in simplest radical form, where a, b, and c are

positive integers. Find $a + b + c$.

Solution: 008.

Let $y/x = k$. We have $y = kx$. The equation $4(x - 2)^2 + y^2 = 4$ can be changed into

the form of $\dfrac{(kx - 2k)^2}{k^2} + \dfrac{(-y)^2}{4} = 1$.

By Cauchy's Inequality, we have

$1 = \dfrac{(kx - 2k)^2}{k^2} + \dfrac{(-y)^2}{4} \geq \dfrac{(kx - 2k - y)^2}{k^2 + 4} = \dfrac{4k^2}{k^2 + 4}$.

Thus $1 \geq \dfrac{4k^2}{k^2 + 4}$ $\Rightarrow$ $k^2 + 4 \geq 4k^2$ $\Rightarrow$ $k^2 \leq \dfrac{4}{3}$.

Solving, we get $k \leq \dfrac{2\sqrt{3}}{3}$ or $k \geq -\dfrac{2\sqrt{3}}{3}$. The smallest value of y/x is $-\dfrac{2\sqrt{3}}{3}$. This

value occurs when $\dfrac{kx - 2k}{k^2} = \dfrac{-y}{4}$, or $x = \mp\dfrac{3}{2}$ and $y = \pm\sqrt{3}$. The answer is $2 + 3$

$+ 3 = 008$.

Example 12. (2005 AIME II Problems 15) Let ω_1 and ω_2 denote the circles $x^2 +$
$y^2 + 10x - 24y - 87 = 0$ and $x^2 + y^2 - 10x - 24y + 153 = 0$, respectively. Let m be
the smallest positive value of a for which the line $y = ax$ contains the center of a

circle that is internally tangent to ω_1 and externally tangent to ω_2. Given that $m^2 = p/q$, where p and q are relatively prime positive integers, find $p + q$.

Solution: 169.

We use the Cauchy inequality to solve the problem.

Complete the squares to obtain $(x + 5)^2 + (y - 12)^2 = 256$ and $(x - 5)^2 + (y - 12)^2 = 16$ for ω_1 and ω_2, respectively.

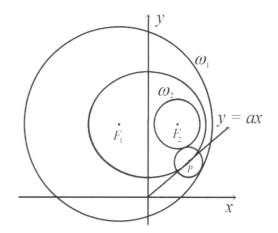

Hence ω_1 is centered at $F_1(-5, 12)$ with radius 16, and ω_1 is centered at $F_2(5, 12)$ with radius 4.

Let P be the center of the third circle, and let r be its radius. Then $PF_1 = 16 - r$ and $PF_2 = 4 + r$. We see that $16 - r + 4 + r = 20$ which is a constant.

Thus P is on the ellipse centered at $(0, 12)$ with foci F_1, F_2 and $PF_1 + PF_2 = 20$.

The major axis is 20 and the minor axis is $\sqrt{20^2 - (5-(-5))^2} = 10\sqrt{3}$. Therefore

the equation of the ellipse is $\dfrac{x^2}{100} + \dfrac{(y-12)^2}{75} = 1$.

By Cauchy, $1 = \dfrac{(-ax)^2}{100a^2} + \dfrac{(y-12)^2}{75} \geq \dfrac{(y - ax - 12)^2}{100a^2 + 75} = \dfrac{(0-12)^2}{100a^2 + 75} = \dfrac{144}{100a^2 + 75}$.

So, we have: $\dfrac{144}{100a^2 + 75} \leq 1 \implies 100a^2 + 75 \geq 144 \implies a^2 \geq \dfrac{69}{100}$.

Thus $m^2 = 69/100$, and $p + q = 169$.

2.3. Proving Inequalities

Example 13. Let $a, b, c, d \geq 0$, show that $\dfrac{1}{a} + \dfrac{1}{b} + \dfrac{4}{c} + \dfrac{16}{d} \geq \dfrac{64}{a+b+c+d}$.

Proof:

$$\frac{1}{a}+\frac{1}{b}+\frac{4}{c}+\frac{16}{d}=\frac{1^2}{a}+\frac{1^2}{b}+\frac{2^2}{c}+\frac{4^2}{d}$$

By Cauchy's (1.3.3): $\dfrac{1^2}{a}+\dfrac{1^2}{b}+\dfrac{2^2}{c}+\dfrac{4^2}{d}\geq\dfrac{(1+1+2+4)^2}{a+b+c+d}=\dfrac{64}{a+b+c+d}.$

Example 14. Show that $\dfrac{a^2}{b+c}+\dfrac{b^2}{c+a}+\dfrac{c^2}{a+b}\geq\dfrac{a+b+c}{2}$ if $a, b, c \in R^+$.

Proof:

By Cauchy's (1.3.3), $\dfrac{a^2}{b+c}+\dfrac{b^2}{c+a}+\dfrac{c^2}{a+b}\geq\dfrac{(a+b+c)^2}{2(a+b+c)}=\dfrac{a+b+c}{2}.$

Example 15. Let a, b, c be positive real numbers. Prove the inequality

$$\frac{a}{b+c}+\frac{b}{c+a}+\frac{c}{a+b}\geq\frac{3}{2}.$$

Proof:
By Cauchy's (1.3.3),

$$\frac{a}{b+c}+\frac{b}{c+a}+\frac{c}{a+b}=\frac{a^2}{ab+bc}+\frac{b^2}{ab+bc}+\frac{c^2}{ac+bc}\geq\frac{(a+b+c)^2}{2(ab+bc+ca)}$$

$$=\frac{a^2+b^2+c^2+2(ab+bc+ca)}{2(ab+bc+ca)}\geq\frac{3(ab+bc+ca)}{2(ab+bc+ca)}=\frac{3}{2}.$$

Note we used the following well-known inequality: $a^2+b^2+c^2\geq ab+bc+ca.$

Example 16. Let a, b, x, y, z be positive real numbers. Prove that

$$\frac{x}{ay+bz}+\frac{y}{az+bx}+\frac{z}{ax+by}\geq\frac{3}{a+b}.$$

Solution:

We have $\dfrac{x}{ay+bz}+\dfrac{y}{az+bx}+\dfrac{z}{ax+by}=\dfrac{x^2}{axy+bxz}+\dfrac{y^2}{ayz+bxy}+\dfrac{z^2}{axz+byz}$.

By Cauchy's (1.3.3),

$$\frac{x}{ay+bz}+\frac{y}{az+bx}+\frac{z}{ax+by}\geq\frac{(x+y+z)^2}{(a+b)(xy+xz+yz)}\geq\frac{3}{a+b}.$$

Example 17. a, b, c are positive numbers. $a+b+c=1$. Prove: $\left(a+\dfrac{1}{a}\right)^2+\left(b+\dfrac{1}{b}\right)^2+\left(c+\dfrac{1}{c}\right)^2\geq\dfrac{100}{3}$.

Solution:

By Cauchy's (1.3.3), we have

$$\left(a+\frac{1}{a}\right)^2+\left(b+\frac{1}{b}\right)^2+\left(c+\frac{1}{c}\right)^2\geq\frac{(a+\frac{1}{a}+b+\frac{1}{b}+c+\frac{1}{c})^2}{1+1+1}=\frac{(1+\frac{1}{a}+\frac{1}{b}+\frac{1}{c})^2}{3}$$

$$(1)$$

By Cauchy's (1.3.3), we have $\dfrac{1}{a}+\dfrac{1}{b}+\dfrac{1}{c}\geq\dfrac{(1+1+1)^2}{a+b+c}=9$ $\quad\quad\quad\quad(2)$

Substituting (2) into (1): $\left(a+\dfrac{1}{a}\right)^2+\left(b+\dfrac{1}{b}\right)^2+\left(c+\dfrac{1}{c}\right)^2\geq\dfrac{(1+9)^2}{3}=\dfrac{100}{3}$.

Example 18. x, y, and z are positive numbers. $x^2+y^2+z^2=1$. Prove:

$$\frac{1}{x^2}+\frac{1}{y^2}+\frac{1}{z^2}+\frac{2(x^3+y^3+z^3)}{xyz}\geq15 .$$

Solution:

$$\frac{1}{x^2}+\frac{1}{y^2}+\frac{1}{z^2}+\frac{2(x^3+y^3+z^3)}{xyz}=\frac{1}{x^2}+\frac{1}{y^2}+\frac{1}{z^2}+(\frac{2x^3}{xyz}+\frac{2y^3}{xyz}+\frac{2z^3}{xyz})$$

$$=\frac{1}{x^2}+\frac{1}{y^2}+\frac{1}{z^2}+2(\frac{x^2}{yz}+\frac{y^2}{xz}+\frac{z^2}{xy}).$$

By Cauchy 1.3.3, $\dfrac{1}{x^2}+\dfrac{1}{y^2}+\dfrac{1}{z^2}\geq\dfrac{(1+1+1)^2}{x^2+y^2+z^2}=9$ (1)

By Cauchy 1.3.3, $\dfrac{x^2}{yz}+\dfrac{y^2}{xz}+\dfrac{z^2}{xy}\geq\dfrac{(x+y+z)^2}{xy+yz+zx}=\dfrac{x^2+y^2+z^2+2(xy+yz+zx)}{xy+yz+zx}$

$$\geq\frac{xy+yz+zx+2(xy+yz+zx)}{xy+yz+zx}=3.$$

So $2(\dfrac{x^2}{yz}+\dfrac{y^2}{xz}+\dfrac{z^2}{xy})\geq6$ (2)

(1) + (2): $\dfrac{1}{x^2}+\dfrac{1}{y^2}+\dfrac{1}{z^2}+\dfrac{2(x^3+y^3+z^3)}{xyz}\geq15$.

Example 19. (IMO) Let a, b, c be positive numbers such that $abc=1$. Prove that

$$\frac{1}{a^3(b+c)}+\frac{1}{b^3(a+c)}+\frac{1}{c^3(a+b)}\geq\frac{3}{2}.$$

Solution:
Method 1:

We see that $\dfrac{1}{a^3(b+c)}+\dfrac{1}{b^3(a+c)}+\dfrac{1}{c^3(a+b)}=\dfrac{\frac{1}{a^2}}{ab+ac}+\dfrac{\frac{1}{b^2}}{ab+bc}+\dfrac{\frac{1}{c^2}}{ac+bc}$.

By Cauchy's (1.3.3), $\dfrac{\frac{1}{a^2}}{ab+ac}+\dfrac{\frac{1}{b^2}}{ab+bc}+\dfrac{\frac{1}{c^2}}{ac+bc}\geq\dfrac{(\frac{1}{a}+\frac{1}{b}+\frac{1}{c})^2}{2(ab+bc+ac)}$.

We know that $abc = 1$, so $\left(\dfrac{1}{a} + \dfrac{1}{b} + \dfrac{1}{c}\right)^2 = \dfrac{(ab + bc + ca)^2}{(abc)^2} = (ab + bc + ca)^2$.

Therefore $\dfrac{1}{a^3(b+c)} + \dfrac{1}{b^3(a+c)} + \dfrac{1}{c^3(a+b)} \geq \dfrac{(ab + bc + ca)}{2} \geq \dfrac{3\sqrt[3]{(abc)^2}}{2} = \dfrac{3}{2}$.

Method 2:

$$\dfrac{1}{a^3(b+c)} + \dfrac{1}{b^3(a+c)} + \dfrac{1}{c^3(a+b)} = \dfrac{(bc)^2}{ab + ac} + \dfrac{(ac)^2}{bc + ba} + \dfrac{(ab)^2}{ac + bc}.$$

By Cauchy's (1.3.3), we have

$$\dfrac{(bc)^2}{ab + ac} + \dfrac{(ac)^2}{bc + ba} + \dfrac{(ab)^2}{ac + bc} \geq \dfrac{(bc + ac + ab)^2}{ab + ac + bc + ba + ac + bc} = \dfrac{1}{2}(ab + bc + ca)$$

By AM-GM, we know that $bc + ca + ab \geq 3\sqrt[3]{(abc)^2} = 3$. So

$$\dfrac{(bc)^2}{ab + ac} + \dfrac{(ac)^2}{bc + ba} + \dfrac{(ab)^2}{ac + bc} \geq \dfrac{1}{2}(ab + bc + ca) \geq \dfrac{1}{2} \cdot 3\sqrt[3]{(abc)^2} = \dfrac{3}{2}.$$

Example 20. (ARML) If a, b, $c > 0$ and $a + b + c = 6$, show that

$(a + \dfrac{1}{b})^2 + (b + \dfrac{1}{c})^2 + (c + \dfrac{1}{a})^2 \geq \dfrac{75}{4}$.

Solution:

$$(a + \dfrac{1}{b})^2 + (b + \dfrac{1}{c})^2 + (c + \dfrac{1}{a})^2 \geq \dfrac{(a + \dfrac{1}{b} + b + \dfrac{1}{c} + c + \dfrac{1}{a})^2}{1 + 1 + 1} = \dfrac{(6 + \dfrac{1}{a} + \dfrac{1}{b} + \dfrac{1}{c})^2}{3} \quad (1)$$

By Cauchy's (1.3.3), we have $\dfrac{1}{a} + \dfrac{1}{b} + \dfrac{1}{c} \geq \dfrac{(1 + 1 + 1)^2}{a + b + c} = \dfrac{9}{6} = \dfrac{3}{2}$ $\quad (2)$

Substituting (2) into (1): $(a + \dfrac{1}{b})^2 + (b + \dfrac{1}{c})^2 + (c + \dfrac{1}{a})^2 \geq \dfrac{(6 + \dfrac{3}{2})^2}{3} = \dfrac{75}{4}$.

PROBLEMS

Problem 1. The smallest value of $3x^2 + 2y^2 + 5z^2$ can be expressed as $\dfrac{m}{n}$, where m and n are positive integers relatively prime. Find $m + n$ if $3x + 4y + 5z = 1$. (x, y, $z \in$ R).

Problem 2 The smallest value of $x^2 + y^2 + z^2$ can be expressed as $\dfrac{m}{n}$, where m and n are positive integers relatively prime. Find $m + n$ if $2x + y + z = 9$. x, y, z are real.

Problem 3. Find the smallest value of $(p + 1)^2 + (q - 3)^2$ if $2p + 3q + 6 = 0$. $p, q \in$ R.

Problem 4. The greatest value of $\sqrt{3a+1} + \sqrt{3b+1} + \sqrt{3c+1}$ can be expressed as $m\sqrt{n}$ in simplest radical form. Find $m + n$ if $a + b + c = 1$.

Problem 5. Find the greatest possible value for a if $\dfrac{1}{x^2} + \dfrac{1}{(a-x)^2} \geq 2$ is always true when $0 < x < a$.

Problem 6. (China Hope Cup) Find the range of $a^2 + b^2 + c^2$ if $a + b + c = 2$, $0 < a, b, c < 1$.

(A) $[\dfrac{4}{3} + \infty)$.   (B) $[\dfrac{4}{3}, 2]$.   (C) $[\dfrac{4}{3}, 2)$.   (D) $(\dfrac{4}{3}, 2)$.

Problem 7. (2000 China Fujian High School Math Contest) $a, b \in R^+$. $a + b = 1$.

Prove: $(a + \dfrac{1}{a})^2 + (b + \dfrac{1}{b})^2 \geq \dfrac{25}{2}$.

Problem 8. Show that $(a-1)^2 + (b-1)^2 \geq \dfrac{9}{2}$ if $a + b + 1 = 0$.

Problem 9. Let $x, y, z > 0$. Prove that $\dfrac{2}{x+y} + \dfrac{2}{y+z} + \dfrac{2}{z+x} \geq \dfrac{9}{x+y+z}$.

Problem 10. Let $a, b, c > 0$. Prove that $\dfrac{a^2+b^2}{a+b} + \dfrac{b^2+c^2}{b+c} + \dfrac{a^2+c^2}{a+c} \geq a+b+c$.

Problem 11. Let $x, y, z > 0$. Prove that

$$\dfrac{x}{x+2y+3z} + \dfrac{y}{y+2z+3x} + \dfrac{z}{z+2x+3y} \geq \dfrac{1}{2}.$$

Problem 12. Let $x, y, z > 0$. Prove that

$$\dfrac{x^2}{(x+y)(x+z)} + \dfrac{y^2}{(y+z)(y+x)} + \dfrac{z^2}{(z+x)(z+y)} \geq \dfrac{3}{4}.$$

Problem 13. The smallest value of $\dfrac{1}{\alpha^2} + \dfrac{1}{\beta^2} + \dfrac{1}{\gamma^2}$ can be expressed as $\dfrac{m}{\pi^2}$, where

if α, β, and γ are three angles in radians of a triangle, and m is a positive integer. What is m?

Problem 14. (ARML) a, b, c, x, y, z are real numbers. $a^2 + b^2 + c^2 = 25$, $x^2 + y^2 + z^2 = 36$, and $ax + by + cz = 30$. $\dfrac{a+b+c}{x+y+z}$ can be expressed as $\dfrac{m}{n}$, where m and n are positive integers relatively prime. Find $m + n$.

Problem 15. (AMC) Given that $x^2 + y^2 = 14x + 6y + 6$, what is the largest possible value that $3x + 4y$ can have?

Problem 16. The equation of a plane is $5x - 2y - z - 20 = 0$. P in the plane is the foot of the perpendicular from the origin to the plane. The x- coordinate of P can be written as $\dfrac{m}{n}$, where m and n are positive integers relatively prime. Find $m + n$.

Problem 17. (China Hope Cup Math Contest Training) Line l: $y = x + 5$ meet x-axis at A and y-axis at B. C is a point on the ellipse $\dfrac{x^2}{16} + \dfrac{y^2}{9} = 1$. What is the greatest possible area of $\triangle ABC$?

Problem 18. The shortest distance from a point on the hyperbola $\dfrac{x^2}{25} - \dfrac{y^2}{9} = 1$ to the line l: $x - y - 3 = 0$ can be written as $\dfrac{\sqrt{m}}{n}$ in simplest radical form. Find $m + n$.

Problem 19. P is a point on the ellipse $\dfrac{x^2}{25}+\dfrac{y^2}{16}=1$ such that the distance from P to the line l: $4x+5y-40=0$ is the shortest. The x-coordinate of P can be written as $\dfrac{s\sqrt{m}}{n}$ in simplest radical from. Find $s+m+n$.

Problem 20. (2002 USAMO) Let ABC be a triangle such that

$$(\cot\frac{A}{2})^2+(2\cot\frac{B}{2})^2+(3\cot\frac{C}{2})^2=(\frac{6s}{7r})^2,$$ where s and r denote its semiperimeter

and its inradius, respectively. Prove that triangle ABC is similar to a triangle T whose side lengths are all positive integers with no common divisor and determine these integers.

Problem 21. (ARML) If a, b, c, and d are each positive, $a+b+c+d=8$, $a^2+b^2+c^2+d^2=25$, and $c=d$, compute the greatest value that c can have.

SOLUTIONS:

Problem 1. Solution: 017.

By Cauchy's 1.3.3,

$$3x^2 + 2y^2 + 5z^2 = \frac{(3x)^2}{3} + \frac{(4y)^2}{8} + \frac{(5z)^2}{5} \geq \frac{(3x+4y+5z)^2}{3+8+5} = \frac{1}{16}.$$

Equality occurs when $x = \frac{y}{2} = z = \frac{1}{16}$. So the smallest value is $\frac{1}{16}$ and $m + n = 17$.

Problem 2. Solution: 029.

By Cauchy's Inequality 1.3.3:

$$x^2 + y^2 + z^2 = \frac{(2x)^2}{4} + y^2 + z^2 \geq \frac{(2x+y+z)^2}{4+1+1} = \frac{27}{2}.$$ The smallest value is $\frac{27}{2}$ and $m + n = 29$.

Equality occurs when $\frac{2x}{4} = \frac{y}{1} = \frac{z}{1}$ or $x = 3$, $y = 3/2$ and $z = 3/2$.

Problem 3. Solution: 013.

$$(p+1)^2 + (q-3)^2 = \frac{(2p+2)^2}{4} + \frac{(3q-9)^2}{9}.$$

By Cauchy's (1.3.3), we have

$$\frac{(2p+2)^2}{4} + \frac{(3q-9)^2}{9} \geq \frac{(2p+2+3q-9)^2}{4+9} = \frac{(-6+2-9)^2}{4+9} = \frac{(-13)^2}{13} = 13.$$

$$\begin{cases} 2p + 3q + 6 = 0 \\ \\ \dfrac{2p+2}{4} = \dfrac{3q-9}{9} \end{cases}$$

Solving the system of equations, we get $p = -3$, and $q = 0$.

Therefore the smallest value is 13 when $p = -3$, and $q = 0$.

Problem 4. Solution: 005.

By Cauchy's Inequality,

$(a_1^2 + a_2^2 + ... + a_n^2) \cdot (b_1^2 + b_2^2 + ... + b_n^2) \geq (a_1 b_1 + a_2 b_2 + ... + a_n b_n)^2$, we have

$(\sqrt{3a+1} \cdot 1 + \sqrt{3b+1} \cdot 1 + \sqrt{3c+1} \cdot 1)^2$

$\leq [(3a+1) + (3b+1) + (3c+1)] \cdot (1^2 + 1^2 + 1^2) = 18$.

Equality occurs when $a = b = c = \dfrac{1}{3}$.

The greatest value of $\sqrt{3a+1} + \sqrt{3b+1} + \sqrt{3c+1}$ is $3\sqrt{2}$. $m + n = 5$.

Problem 5. Solution: 002.

By Cauchy's inequality 1.3.2: $\dfrac{x_1^2}{y_1} + \dfrac{x_2^2}{y_2} \geq \dfrac{(x_1 + x_2)^2}{y_1 + y_2}$, we have

$\dfrac{1}{x} + \dfrac{1}{a-x} \geq \dfrac{4}{a}$

$\qquad$ (1)

Squaring both sides of (1): $(\dfrac{1}{x} + \dfrac{1}{a-x})^2 \geq (\dfrac{4}{a})^2$

$\Rightarrow \quad \dfrac{1}{x^2} + \dfrac{1}{(a-x)^2} + 2 \cdot \dfrac{1}{x(a-x)} \geq (\dfrac{4}{a})^2$

$\qquad$ (2)

We know that by AM-GM: $\dfrac{1}{x^2} + \dfrac{1}{(a-x)^2} \geq 2 \cdot \sqrt{\dfrac{1}{x^2 \cdot (a-x)^2}} = 2 \dfrac{1}{x} \cdot \dfrac{1}{a-x}$.

If we replace $2 \cdot \dfrac{1}{x(a-x)}$ by $\dfrac{1}{x^2} + \dfrac{1}{(a-x)^2}$, the inequality is still true.

Thus, (2) becomes $2(\dfrac{1}{x^2} + \dfrac{1}{(a-x)^2}) \geq (\dfrac{4}{a})^2 \Rightarrow \dfrac{1}{x^2} + \dfrac{1}{(a-x)^2} \geq \dfrac{8}{a^2}$

Equality occurs when $x = \dfrac{a}{2}$.

From $\dfrac{8}{a^2} \geq 2$, we get $0 < a \leq 2$. $\therefore a_{\max} = 2$. The greatest possible value for

a is 2.

Problem 6. Solution: (C).

By Cauchy's (1.3.3): $a^2 + b^2 + c^2 \geq \dfrac{(a+b+c)^2}{1+1+1} = \dfrac{4}{3}$.

So $a^2 + b^2 + c^2 \geq \dfrac{4}{3}$.

We also know that $0 < a, b, c < 1$.

We can have $(1-a)(1-b)(1-c) > 0 \Rightarrow$ $1 - (a+b+c) + (ab+bc+ca) - abc$

> 0.

So $ab + bc + ca > 1$.

Thus $a^2 + b^2 + c^2 = (a+b+c)^2 - 2(ab+bc+ca)$

$= 4 - 2(ab+bc+ca) < 4 - 2 = 2$.

The answer is $\dfrac{4}{3} \leq a^2 + b^2 + c^2 < 2$.

Problem 7. Solution:

By Cauchy's Inequality, we have

$(a+\dfrac{1}{a})^2 + (b+\dfrac{1}{b})^2 \geq \dfrac{1}{2}[(a+\dfrac{1}{a}) + (b+\dfrac{1}{b})]^2 = \dfrac{1}{2}[1+(\dfrac{1}{a}+\dfrac{1}{b})]^2$

but $\dfrac{1}{a} + \dfrac{1}{b} = (a+b)\,(\dfrac{1}{a}+\dfrac{1}{b}) \geq 2\sqrt{ab} \cdot 2\sqrt{\dfrac{1}{a}\cdot\dfrac{1}{b}} = 4$.

Therefore $(a+\dfrac{1}{a})^2 + (b+\dfrac{1}{b})^2 \geq \dfrac{1}{2}(1+4)^2 = \dfrac{25}{2}$.

Problem 8. Solution:

By Cauchy's (1.3.3), $(a-1)^2 + (b-1)^2 \ge \dfrac{(a-1+b-1)^2}{2} = \dfrac{(a+b-2)^2}{2}$

$= \dfrac{(-1-2)^2}{2}$, or

$(a-1)^2 + (b-1)^2 \ge \dfrac{9}{2}$.

Problem 9. Solution:

Writing the left-hand side as $\dfrac{(\sqrt{2})^2}{x+y} + \dfrac{(\sqrt{2})^2}{y+z} + \dfrac{(\sqrt{2})^2}{z+x}$.

By Cauchy's (1.3.3), $\dfrac{(\sqrt{2})^2}{x+y} + \dfrac{(\sqrt{2})^2}{y+z} + \dfrac{(\sqrt{2})^2}{z+x} \ge \dfrac{(3\sqrt{2})^2}{2(x+y+z)} = \dfrac{9}{x+y+z}$.

Equality occurs when $x = y = z$.

Problem 10. Solution:

We write the left-hand side as

$\dfrac{a^2}{a+b} + \dfrac{b^2}{b+c} + \dfrac{c^2}{a+c} + \dfrac{b^2}{a+b} + \dfrac{c^2}{b+c} + \dfrac{a^2}{a+c}$.

By Cauchy's (1.3.3), $\dfrac{a^2+b^2}{a+b} + \dfrac{b^2+c^2}{b+c} + \dfrac{a^2+c^2}{a+c} \ge \dfrac{(2a+2b+2c)^2}{4(a+b+c)} = a+b+c$.

Problem 11. Solution:

We write the left-hand side as

$\dfrac{x^2}{x^2+2xy+3xz} + \dfrac{y^2}{y^2+2yz+3xy} + \dfrac{z^2}{z^2+2xz+3yz}$

By Cauchy's (1.3.3), we have

$\dfrac{x}{x+2y+3z} + \dfrac{y}{y+2z+3x} + \dfrac{z}{z+2x+3y} \ge \dfrac{(x+y+z)^2}{x^2+y^2+z^2+5(xy+xz+yz)}$.

We know that $x^2 + y^2 + z^2 \geq xy + xz + yz$.

It follows that

$$\frac{(x+y+z)^2}{x^2 + y^2 + z^2 + 5(xy + xz + yz)} \geq \frac{1}{2}, \text{ and}$$

$$\frac{x}{x+2y+3z} + \frac{y}{y+2z+3x} + \frac{z}{z+2x+3y} \geq \frac{1}{2}.$$

Problem 12. Solution:
By Cauchy's (1.3.3), we have

$$\frac{x^2}{(x+y)(x+z)} + \frac{y^2}{(y+z)(y+x)} + \frac{z^2}{(z+x)(z+y)} \geq \frac{(x+y+z)^2}{x^2 + y^2 + z^2 + 3(xy + xz + yz)}.$$

We know that $x^2 + y^2 + z^2 \geq xy + xz + yz$.

It follows that $\dfrac{(x+y+z)^2}{x^2 + y^2 + z^2 + 3(xy + xz + yz)} \geq \dfrac{3}{4}$, or

$$\frac{x^2}{(x+y)(x+z)} + \frac{y^2}{(y+z)(y+x)} + \frac{z^2}{(z+x)(z+y)} \geq \frac{3}{4}.$$

Problem 13. Solution: 027.
We know that $x^2 + y^2 + z^2 \geq xy + yz + zx$

If we let $\dfrac{1}{\alpha} = x$, $\dfrac{1}{\beta} = y$, and $\dfrac{1}{\gamma} = z$, we will be able to above inequality to get:

$$\frac{1}{\alpha^2} + \frac{1}{\beta^2} + \frac{1}{\gamma^2} \geq \frac{1}{\alpha\beta} + \frac{1}{\beta\gamma} + \frac{1}{\gamma\alpha} \tag{1}$$

By Cauchy's (1.3.3): $\dfrac{1}{\alpha\beta} + \dfrac{1}{\beta\gamma} + \dfrac{1}{\gamma\alpha} \geq \dfrac{(1+1+1)^2}{\alpha\beta + \beta\gamma + \gamma\alpha}$ \hfill (2)

We know that $(\alpha + \beta + \gamma)^2 = \alpha^2 + \beta^2 + \gamma^2 + 2(\alpha\beta + \beta\gamma + \gamma\alpha) \geq 3(\alpha\beta + \beta\gamma + \gamma\alpha)$.

$$\frac{(\alpha + \beta + \gamma)^2}{3} \geq \alpha\beta + \beta\gamma + \gamma\alpha \tag{3}$$

Substituting (3) into (2), we get: $\dfrac{1}{\alpha\beta} + \dfrac{1}{\beta\gamma} + \dfrac{1}{\gamma\alpha} \geq \dfrac{(1+1+1)^2}{\dfrac{(\alpha + \beta + \gamma)^2}{3}} = \dfrac{27}{\pi^2}$.

Equality occurs when $\alpha + \beta + \gamma = \dfrac{\pi}{3}$. The smallest value of $\dfrac{1}{\alpha^2} + \dfrac{1}{\beta^2} + \dfrac{1}{\gamma^2}$ is $\dfrac{27}{\pi^2}$.

So $m = 27$.

Problem 14. Solution: 011.

By Cauchy's,

$(a^2 + b^2 + c^2)(x^2 + y^2 + z^2) \geq (ax + by + z)^2$. Plugging in the given values in the

problem, this inequality becomes $25 \times 36 \geq 30^2$, which is true.

Equality occurs when $\dfrac{a}{x} = \dfrac{b}{y} = \dfrac{c}{z} = k \Rightarrow a = kx, b = ky, c = kz$.

$a^2 + b^2 + c^2 = k^2(x^2 + y^2 + z^2) \Rightarrow k^2 = \dfrac{25}{36}$ (ignoring the negative value).

Therefore $\dfrac{a + b + c}{x + y + z} = k = \dfrac{5}{6}$. $m + n = 11$.

Problem 15. Solution: 073.

(1996 AMC problem #25). There are two official solutions to this problem. Here
we provide a third solution of our own.

The equation $x^2 + y^2 = 14x + 6y + 6$ can be written as $(x - 7)^2 + (y - 3)^2 = 8^2$.

    (1)

We can further write the equation in the form of

$$\frac{(3x - 21)^2}{3^2} + \frac{(4y - 12)^2}{4^2} = 8^2$$

    (2)

Applying Cauchy's (1.3.2) to the left hand side of (2):

$$\frac{(3x-21)^2}{3^2}+\frac{(4x-12)^2}{4^2}\geq\frac{(3x-21+4y-12)^2}{3^2+4^2}=\frac{(3x+4y-33)^2}{5^2}.$$

So we have $8^2\geq\dfrac{(3x+4y-33)^2}{5^2}$ $\quad\Rightarrow\quad$ $5^2\cdot 8^2\geq(3x+4y-33)^2$.

Since we want the largest value of $3x + 4y$, we can take the square root of both sides of the above inequality and obtain

$$5\cdot 8\geq 3x+4y-33 \quad\Rightarrow\quad 73\geq 3x+4y.$$

Equality occurs when $\dfrac{3x-21}{3^2}=\dfrac{4y-12}{4^2}$ $\quad\Rightarrow\quad$ $\dfrac{x-7}{3}=\dfrac{y-3}{4}$ $\quad\Rightarrow\quad$

$$x-7=\frac{3}{4}(y-3)$$
$$(3)$$

Substituting (3) into (1), we have

$$\frac{4^2(y-3)^2}{3^2}+(y-3)^2=8^2 \quad\Rightarrow\quad \frac{5^2(y-3)^2}{3^2}=8^2 \quad\Rightarrow\quad y=\frac{47}{5}, \text{ and}$$

$$x=\frac{59}{5}.$$

It follows that the largest value of $3x + 4y$ is 73.

Problem 16. Solution: 013.

Let the coordinates of P be (x, y, z).

The distance from the origin to the plane is $d=\sqrt{x^2+y^2+z^2}$.

By Cauchy, $x^2+y^2+z^2=\dfrac{(5x)^2}{25}+\dfrac{(-2y)^2}{4}+\dfrac{(-z)^2}{1}\geq\dfrac{(5x-2y-z)^2}{25+4+1}=\dfrac{20^2}{30}=\dfrac{40}{3}$.

Equality holds when $\dfrac{5x}{25}=\dfrac{-2y}{4}=\dfrac{-z}{1}$ $\quad\Rightarrow\quad$ $x=-5z$ and $y=2z$.

So $5x-2y-z-20=0$ $\quad\Rightarrow\quad$ $5(-5z)-2(2z)-z=20$

$z = -\dfrac{2}{3}$, $y = -\dfrac{4}{3}$, and $x = \dfrac{10}{3}$. $m + n = 13$.

Note that the distance from the point (x_1, y_1, z_1) to the plane $ax + by + cz + d = 0$

can also be calculated by $\dfrac{|ax_1 + by_1 + cz_1 + d|}{\sqrt{a^2 + b^2 + c^2}}$.

Problem 17. Solution: 25.
Method 1 (official solution):
Let the coordinate of C be $C(4\cos\theta, 3\sin\theta)$.

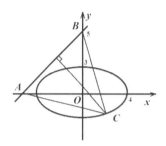

The distance from C to l: $d = \dfrac{|5\cos(\theta + \varphi) + 5|}{\sqrt{2}}$. The greatest

value of d is $\dfrac{10}{\sqrt{2}}$ when $\cos(\theta + \varphi) = 1$.

Applying Pythagorean Theorem in right triangle AOB we get: $|AB| = 5\sqrt{2}$. We

know that $S_{\triangle ABC} = \dfrac{1}{2}|AB|d$. Therefore $(S_{\triangle ABC})_{max} = \dfrac{1}{2} \times 5\sqrt{2} \times \dfrac{10}{\sqrt{2}} = 25$.

Method 2 (our solution):
We want to find the greatest area of $\triangle ABC$. The length of AB is constant. So we
want to have the greatest value for the height (the distance from C to the line AB).

$d = \dfrac{|x - y + 5|}{\sqrt{1^2 + (-1)^2}} = \dfrac{|x - y + 5|}{\sqrt{2}}$.

We want to find the greatest value of $x - y$.

By Cauchy, $1 = \dfrac{x^2}{16} + \dfrac{y^2}{9} = \dfrac{x^2}{16} + \dfrac{(-y)^2}{9} \geq \dfrac{(x - y)^2}{16 + 9} = \dfrac{(x - y)^2}{25}$.

So $(x - y)^2 \leq 25 \qquad \Rightarrow \qquad x - y \leq 5$.

The greatest value of $x - y$ is 5. Equality occurs when $\dfrac{x}{16} = \dfrac{-y}{9}$, or $x = \dfrac{16}{5}$ and

$y = -\dfrac{9}{5}$.

So the greatest value of d is $\dfrac{10}{\sqrt{2}}$. Therefore $(S_{\triangle ABC})_{max} = \dfrac{1}{2} \times 5\sqrt{2} \times \dfrac{10}{\sqrt{2}} = 25$.

Problem 18. Solution: 004.

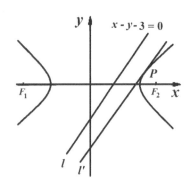

Method 1:

When $l: x - y - 3 = 0$ is sliding right to be tangent to the hyperbola, the distance from a point to the line l is the smallest, which is the distance between two parallel lines.

Let $l': x - y - m = 0$, then $l' /\!/ l$.

Substituting $y = x - m$ into the hyperbola, we get

$16x^2 - 50mx + 25m^2 + 225 = 0$.

So $\Delta = (50m)^2 - 4 \times 16 \times (25m^2 + 225) = 0$.

Solving, we get $m = 4$, and $m = -4$ (we can ignore this value).

Thus $l': x - y - 4 = 0$.

The distance between two lines is $\dfrac{|-3 + 4|}{\sqrt{2}} = \dfrac{\sqrt{2}}{2}$, so the shortest distance is $\dfrac{\sqrt{2}}{2}$.

$m + n = 4$.

Method 2 (our solution):

The distance from a point on the hyperbola to the line is

$$d = \frac{|x - y - 3|}{\sqrt{1^2 + (-1)^2}} = \frac{|x - y - 3|}{\sqrt{2}}.$$

The smallest distance d is obtained when $x - y$ is as close to 3 as possible.

$$1 = \frac{x^2}{25} - \frac{y^2}{9} = \frac{x^2}{25} + \frac{(-y)^2}{-9} \geq \frac{(x - y)^2}{25 - 9} = \frac{(x - y)^2}{16} \qquad \Rightarrow \qquad 16 \geq (x - y)^2.$$

The closest possible value of $x - y$ is 4, which is achieved when $\dfrac{x}{25} = \dfrac{-y}{-9}$.

Solving the system of equations:

$$\begin{cases} 9x = 25y \\ x - y = 4 \end{cases}$$

we get $x = 25/4$ and $y = 9/4$.

$$d = \frac{|x - y - 3|}{\sqrt{1^2 + (-1)^2}} = \frac{|x - y - 3|}{\sqrt{2}} = \frac{|4 - 3|}{\sqrt{2}} = \frac{1}{\sqrt{2}} = \frac{\sqrt{2}}{2} . \ m + n = 4.$$

Problem 19. Solution: 009.

The distance from a point on the ellipse to the line is

$$d = \frac{|4x + 5y - 40|}{\sqrt{4^2 + 5^2}} = \frac{|4x + 5y - 40|}{\sqrt{41}} .$$

We want to find the smallest value of d. So we want to find the greatest value of $4x + 5y$ so the numerator could be the smallest.

We rewrite $\dfrac{x^2}{25} + \dfrac{y^2}{16} = 1$ as $\dfrac{(4x)^2}{25 \times 4^2} + \dfrac{(5y)^2}{16 \times 5^2} = 1$.

By Cauchy, $\dfrac{(4x)^2}{25 \times 4^2} + \dfrac{(5y)^2}{16 \times 5^2} \geq \dfrac{(4x + 5y)^2}{25 \cdot 16 + 16 \cdot 25} = \dfrac{(4x + 5y)^2}{800}$.

Thus $1 \geq \dfrac{(4x + 5y)^2}{800}$. So $(4x + 5y)^2 \leq 800 \quad \Rightarrow \quad 4x + 5y \leq 20\sqrt{2}$.

The greatest value of $4x + 5y$ is $20\sqrt{2}$.

Equality occurs when $\dfrac{4x}{400} = \dfrac{5y}{400}$, or $x = \dfrac{5}{2}\sqrt{2}$ and $y = 2\sqrt{2}$. So $s + m + n = 5 + 2 + 2 = 9$.

Note that the shortest distance is $d = \dfrac{20\sqrt{2} - 40}{\sqrt{41}}$.

Problem 20. Solution:

We know that $\cot \dfrac{A}{2} = \dfrac{s - a}{r}$, $\cot \dfrac{B}{2} = \dfrac{s - b}{r}$, $\cot \dfrac{C}{2} = \dfrac{s - c}{r}$.

So $(\cot\frac{A}{2})^2 + (2\cot\frac{B}{2})^2 + (3\cot\frac{C}{2})^2 = (\frac{6s}{7r})^2$ can be written as

$$(s-a)^2 + 2^2(s-b)^2 + 3^2(s-c)^2 = (\frac{6s}{7})^2 \qquad (1)$$

From the following we see that (1) is the case of Cauchy inequality when the equality holds.

$$\frac{(s-a)^2}{1} + \frac{(s-b)^2}{\frac{1}{4}} + \frac{(s-c)^2}{\frac{1}{9}} \geq \frac{(s-a+s-b+s-c)^2}{1+\frac{1}{4}+\frac{1}{9}} = (\frac{6s}{7})^2$$

$$\frac{(s-a)}{1} = \frac{(s-b)}{\frac{1}{4}} = \frac{(s-c)}{\frac{1}{9}} = \frac{(3s-a-b-c)}{1+\frac{1}{4}+\frac{1}{9}} = \frac{36s}{49} \quad \Rightarrow \quad \frac{a}{13} = \frac{b}{40} = \frac{c}{45}.$$

So triangle ABC is similar to a triangle with side lengths 13, 40, 45.

Problem 21. Solution: $\dfrac{7}{2}$.

Let the four numbers be a,b,c,d .

We have $a+b = 8-2c$, and $a^2+b^2 = 25-2c^2$.

By Cauchy's Inequality,

$$a^2+b^2 = \frac{a^2}{1} + \frac{b^2}{1} \geq \frac{(a+b)^2}{1+1} \text{, or } (a+b)^2 \leq 2(a^2+b^2).$$

Since $a+b = 8-2c$ and $a^2+b^2 = 25-2c^2$, we have

$$(8-2c)^2 \leq 2(25-2c^2) \Rightarrow 8c^2 - 32c + 14 \leq 0 \Rightarrow \qquad 4c^2 - 16c + 7 \leq 0 \Rightarrow$$

$$\frac{1}{2} \leq c \leq \frac{7}{2} \text{。 The greatest value of } c \text{ is } \frac{7}{2} \text{ when } a = b = \frac{1}{2}.$$

Made in United States
Troutdale, OR
12/26/2023

16424666R00084